TIME & TIDE

STORIES SHAPED BY THE PASSAGE OF TIME

Ami Dedhia, Amit Suri, Anannya Sane, Anjana Chabria, Arati Raval, Archana Maru Nanda, Avani Shah, Bhavini Furia, Bijal Pratik Shah, Bijal Shah-Chokshi, Chandni Bhatnagar, Dr. Ekta Bhatia, Gayatri Hingorani, Jay Solanki, Kajal Mehra, Kaushal Patel, Kinjal Mehta, Krina Gala, Kruti Sharma, Madhuja Banerjee, Mamta Agarwal, Manasvi Mehta, Manika Tibriwal, Manisha Divan, Meghana Chandrachud, Monaaz Bamji, Nidhi Shah, Nily Mehta, Nirali Hathi, Parizad Srivastava, Payal Shah, Rita Choudhari, Saloni Chheda, Shreya Khosla, Dr. Usha Jayachandran, Vandana Narang Lund, Dr. Vani Parekh, Vijay Lalla, Yūgen, Zeyd Ladha

Edited by Amit Suri

TWAGAA

HTTPS://TWAGAA.COM

First published in 2025 by

TWAGAA

HTTPS://TWAGAA.COM

TWAGAA INTERNATIONAL

Mumbai (Maharashtra), India

Email: hello@twagaa.com

Website: https://twagaa.com

Cover Design by Sucharita Suri (https://sucharitas.world)

Book Typeset at Seek Red (https://seekred.com)

TIME & TIDE - Stories shaped by the passage of time

ISBN eBook: 978-81-991736-5-1

Paperback: 978-81-991736-3-7

10 9 8 7 6 5 4 3 2 1

Contents

Preface

Since the beginning of civilisation, it is stories, relationships, and collaborations that have bound us together and propelled us forward. Around firesides, in temples, schools, and family courtyards, stories have not only entertained but also preserved memory, taught wisdom, and inspired new beginnings. As Margaret Atwood once wrote, *"In the end, we'll all become stories."* This anthology stands as a testament to that truth.

The contributors to *TIME & TIDE* have given us tales that shimmer with authenticity and imagination. Arati Raval's *It'll Pass* blends humour with the fragility of life, while Manisha Divan's *Sol Kadhi – Curry for the Soul* stirs memory through taste, reminding us how food keeps families alive in spirit. In Parizad Srivastava's *3-6-9-12*, love drifts across decades, while Kinjal Mehta's *The Empty Nest* holds the ache of ageing and loss. From Chandni Bhatnagar's spirited *Women in Uniform* to Avani Shah's *Stained With Turmeric and Time*, we see the power of resilience in uniform, in kitchens, and in hearts.

Other voices reflect transformation across tides of change: Anjana Chabria's *Tidewalk* walks us through vulnerability and healing; Manika Tibriwal's comic *Time, Tide & Tapan* finds redemption in chaos; Vijay Lalla's *Myrna and the River of Change* charts empathy's ripple effect. From quiet domesticity in *The Window Seat* (Payal Shah) to the luminous legacy of *The Queen of the Sea* (Bhavini Furia), each story echoes universal truths.

Real-life projects such as this show us the importance of collective creation. Harnessing diverse imaginations – whether in Meghana Chandrachud's *A Vacation, A Lost Phone & The Miracle of Midnight* or Krina Gala's *Checkmating Chaos*

– fuels creativity and ignites sparks in our youth to dream, collaborate, and build legacies. Together, these voices mirror Winston Churchill's reminder that *"We make a living by what we get, but we make a life by what we give."*

TIME & TIDE is more than a collection of tales; it is a celebration of voices, perspectives, and hearts. What makes this anthology truly special is not only the diversity of its stories but the spirit of collaboration that has brought together 40 contributors into one shared journey. In the making of this book, stories were written, yes, but friendships were also formed, ideas exchanged, and bonds strengthened. And now, with every page turned, these 40 names stand side by side, bound together for all time to come. *Isn't that beautiful?*

Such projects are not just about producing books — they are about preserving moments, building legacies, and reminding us that together we truly are Great, Amazing, and Awesome. TWAGAA take pride in bringing like-minded people together to share their stories, whether fiction or non-fiction, and in helping them realise their potential as writers – and as civilisation-builders. The very name TWAGAA says it best: *Together We Are Great, Amazing, and Awesome!*

To every writer – parents, teachers, alumni, and ex-parents of Jamnabai Narsee School – thank you for giving your time, heart, and truth. You have helped make a legacy of anthology with stories that will live far beyond these pages, and may the relationships built here endure even farther. Thank you for your courage, your creativity, and your generosity.

Amit Suri
Editor & Publisher, Mumbai

1

The Queen of the Sea - Samudrarani

~ Bhavini Furia

The jingling of my anklets mocked me with every step. Chink-chink-chink. Like coins being counted. Which, in truth, was all they were.

"Stand straight," the broker hissed as we approached the white mansion. His grip on my elbow left bruises that would bloom purple by morning. "And for God's sake, stop crying. You're not going to your funeral."

But I was. The girl who played with clay dolls and climbed mango trees was being buried today. In her place stood a child-woman draped in a red sari three sizes too large, the fabric swallowing my bony frame whole. The silver anklets – my mother's final gift – bit into my flesh with every trembling step.

"They'll keep you grounded," Ma had whispered as she fastened them, her tears mixing with the turmeric paste she rubbed into the straps. Her hands smelled of cumin and worry. "No matter how far the sea takes you, these will always bring you home."

She lied.

The broker exchanged me for a money purse that clinked much like my anklets. Ramesh-babu barely glanced at his new purchase before waving me toward the kitchen. His three motherless children stared with varying degrees of hostility and curiosity. The eldest – a boy just my age – sniffed. "She doesn't even know how to cook."

That night, after scrubbing pots until my fingers bled, I ran. Not toward the village road (where would I go?), but to the black expanse beyond the mansion's gates – the sea.

Salt spray stung my face as I collapsed onto the wet sand. The waves roared in a language I somehow understood. It said what no one else had since I arrived: *Welcome home.*

Monsoon season taught me the sea's true nature.

On the anniversary of my 'wedding', Ramesh-babu brought home his new wife – a plump, fair-skinned girl from the city who giggled when the children called me 'aunty'. That night, I stole a bottle of coconut arrack from the kitchen and waded into the storm-lashed waves.

The ocean welcomed me like a wrathful god.

Saltwater filled my nose, my mouth, my lungs as the undertow dragged me down. My waterlogged sari twisted around my legs like a shroud. The anklets glowed eerily in the depths, pulling me deeper even as my consciousness faded.

Let go, the current whispered. It's easier this way.

Then – a flash of silver. My mother's face appeared in front, her lips moving soundlessly: "The sea doesn't take victims. Only volunteers."

I kicked upward with a strength I didn't know I possessed, breaching the surface just as lightning split the sky. The waves deposited me on shore like discarded garbage.

When the cook found me at dawn, seaweed in my hair and

sand in my teeth, she crossed herself. "Only witches survive the sea's anger," she muttered angrily under her breath.

I smiled for the first time in a year.

Decades passed. The sea became my confessor, my co-conspirator, my only lover.

I learned it has many moods.

In the morning, the best part of my day, the morning tide with its gentle lapping, helped me steal moments of peace before the household awoke.

At Noon, the crashing waves echoed my rage when Ramesh's son 'accidentally' spilled hot tea on my hands.

At midnight, the midnight murmurs and whispers carried stories of distant lands I'd never seen, except had only dreamt of.

When the doctor declared my womb 'barren,' I didn't weep in his clinic. I waited until midnight, then swam out past the breakers. Floating on my back beneath a star-strewn sky, I let the saltwater carry my tears away. The anklets – now tarnished with age – flashed beneath the surface like drowned coins.

"You're enough," the sea murmured, rocking me in its embrace. "You've always been enough." And this moment I learnt to embrace my solitude.

Years went by. At sixty, I became a legend.

Fishermen left offerings of jasmine and coconuts at my gate. Children dared each other to touch my shadow. The villagers called me "Samudra Devi" – Goddess of the Sea – and spun wild tales: that I could calm storms by singing to the waves. That sharks circled protectively when I swam. That my anklets were forged from melted-down pirate treasure.

The truth was simpler: The sea and I had grown old together. Its waves knew the contours of my grief better than any human ever had.

Then came the drought.

For ninety-three days, no rain fell. Wells turned to dust. The sea receded, leaving behind stinking piles of dead fish and a shoreline studded with bleached bones. Desperate fishermen began whispering about sacrifices.

On the ninety-fourth morning, I walked into the water fully clothed, my mother's anklets shining against my withered skin. The crowd on shore held its breath as I raised my arms – not in surrender, but in invitation.

"Take what you need," I told the sea.

A wave surged higher than any in memory, swallowing me whole. For one glorious moment, I was twelve again – weightless, boundless, free. Then the current spat me back onto the sand, coughing up seawater and laughter.

Behind me, the villagers erupted into cheers as the first raindrops began to fall.

Today, a new sound mingles with the waves – the high, bright laughter of children.

The little girl in the red frock returns every Sunday, her small feet leaving perfect prints in the damp sand. She brings me shells and calls me 'Ajji' – grandmother – though we share no blood.

"Tell me about the storm again!" she demands, plopping onto my porch with the confidence of youth.

I adjust the shawl around my shoulders – threadbare now,

like me – and begin the familiar tale. As I speak, my fingers stray to the anklets, their silver worn smooth by salt and time. The sea murmurs its approval, a timeless echo beneath my words.

Some loves are loud. Ours was the quiet kind – the kind that survives storms and droughts and the slow erosion of years. The kind that endures. The world will not even know I existed, but the sea will always love me and miss me when I have gone.

The sea whispered my name like a lullaby, the anklet chimed in my ears, and never left me alone.

That fine day, my final breath was cradled in the lap of the sea, guarded by the chime of my anklet, when I became one with waves, undisturbed, eternal, finally at home.

~

2

It'll Pass

~ Arati Raval

It's 8 A.M. – otherwise known as the war zone that is school bus pick-up time. *"Have you changed? Have you prayed? Are you ready? The bus is almost here!"* I screamed in the general direction of where my kids should've been. No answer.

"DID YOU HEAR ME?" I scream again. From a totally unexpected corner of the house, my 8 and 6-year-olds Abeer and Nitya emerge, pulling at each other's hair. They were still in their towels. I could feel a painful stab in my chest. *"This 8 A.M. anxiety is going to kill me someday!"* I dismissed.

I rush them through the clothes. Ramble through the mantras. The stab is now a pounding. As they leisurely wear their shoes, I reprimand them. *"Same story every day! You guys just never learn!"* I herd them out the door and punch the lift button. My chest completely clenches. I want to scream, but I am unable to even move.

Oh God, not now! This isn't the right time to die! Not before they catch the bus... which is just around the corner.

THUD!

Darkness.

I wake up in the hospital. The beep of machines. The mayhem of an operating room. It looks big, and expensive.

"Oh no! Is this Hinduja? Had I paid my insurance premium?!"

A doctor hovers over my face. *"I am administering general anaesthesia. Can you count backwards from 10 for me?"*

Count backwards? Right now, I could barely count at all! Whoever comes up with these nonsense ways to...

"Count for me, please?!" the doctor sternly reminds me.

I hesitantly begin *"10, 9, 8..."*

Darkness. (That's the second time in a day now!)

I am in a beautiful garden. Manicured green grass. Clean air. Rainbows in the sky. The fragrance of real jasmine. I wonder why the flowers that we see at Bombay signals never smell good. Rumour has it that they're picked from graveyards, but we'll never know.

As I walk on the soft grass, I hear music. I follow it and find myself at a garden party. Stalls of pav bhaaji and pasta, wine and cheese, ice creams and waffles. Everyone seems happy. Which, of course, means that this can't be real life. *"Gosh! Am I dead?"*

"This way, please," a happy young lady leads me to the noisiest corner of the grounds. As I get closer, it gets louder. Somehow, I recognise these voices. In the uncanny way in which we recognise the sounds of our home. I think, *"That sounds like..."* The lady adds, *"Your family, yes. All the dead ones, at least."*

Then I see him, my Mota Bapa (great-grandfather). I first notice his watch. A vintage HMT, older than time itself. It reads 3:47. I stiffen up, like I always did around him. I tell myself, *"I don't think he even recognises me. Maybe I should just walk past to save him the embarrassment?"*

"Of course, I recognise you. You have your father's samosa nose. All these centuries of evolution, and nature couldn't fix ugly noses!" he snaps.

How did he know what I was thinking?

"We can read thoughts here," he helpfully adds.

"But... I can't read yours," I argue.

"Because you're not one of us."

I am confused. *"So am I not dead?"*

"Not yet, my sweetheart. And I don't think you should be, for a while," said the sweetest voice I'd recognise anywhere in the world. Dadima (grandma)!

I run to hug her. I smell the comfort of her arms. When I kiss her, I feel the softness of her old, wrinkled skin. Oh, I feel at home! She is wearing the watch I had gifted on her 85th birthday. But... her time reads 1:45. What?

But I have more pressing questions.

"How are you? Is this heaven? Please tell me Piyush Kaka didn't make it here. Surely, he went to hell! He hated everybody!" I rattle off.

"No, I didn't!" came Kaka's unmistakable voice. *"I was just unhappy with myself and was projecting it on all of you"*

He recognises my look of utter shock.

"I've been going to therapy and it has been... revealing", he explains.

Despite my indestructible disdain for him, I was relieved that Piyush Kaka didn't hate me. Just when I thought that I could get used to this,

"Oh my God, is that you, Baby?" Yup, now you know. 'Baby'

is my nickname. It's like no one even tried. 35 years later, Baby has her own babies, yet she's still Baby to the family.

"Are those dark circles? And white hair strands? How old are you? You came here before your mumma? You were always the mean one!" Jayshree Maasi rambles, true to character.

It is kind of comforting to know that even death can't change some people. Out of curiosity, I check the time on Jayshree Maasi's wristwatch. 6:30. OK, this is weird.

Dadima smiles as she patiently observes me take it all in.

"Have questions?" she asks.

"Lots!", I exclaim.

"Come," Daadima kindly nods.

She leads me towards a table on the far side, where refreshments await us. I see that she walks just like she did in her last days – with difficulty, but without the pain.

We settle into comfortable chairs. She offers me tea. I take a sip and it feels like heaven. But wait... wasn't I already in heaven?

Daadima laughs. *"You were always full of questions. So come on, shoot."*

"Why is the time different on everyone's watches?" I ask.

"Because we're all stuck in the time of our death."

It hit me like the reveal of 'The Sixth Sense'. I didn't see that coming, even though I should've.

"Why am I here? Am I dead?" I ask.

"Not yet. But you can choose."

"I can choose if I want to die?"

"Only some lucky ones get that choice. So don't squander it."

"I don't want to go back. This place is so much better! The air, the grass, the tea!"

Dadima smiles. *"At first sight, it sure is. We have no jobs to rush to, no errands to run. But we don't have what you have"*

"Chaos, taxes and traffic?" I ask.

"Time, possibilities and life," she says.

I was expecting a joke, not pearls of wisdom.

"Why have you not been going to the gym?" she asks.

"Where's the time, Daadima?"

"No time to take care of yourself?"

She's right. Since I can't defend, I deflect.

"How did you know? Can you see us?"

"They live stream your lives for us," she adds.

"Everything?" I ask, afraid of the answer.

"Let's not go there. Tell me, what were your last words to your husband and kids this morning?" she demands.

Jay was in Delhi on work and had called to check in. I remember I was feeding the kids, so I just quipped, *"Not now! I'll call you later!"*

And then I think of what I told the kids as we waited for the lift. *"You guys just never learn!"*

"Do you want those to be your last words to them?" Daadima searches my face.

"We take our loved ones for granted and instead waste our energy getting the approval of people we don't even like. Isn't that a shame? I mean, I never wore red after your Dada died, because

I was worried about that dimwit Ganga Foi's jeers. Then she goes on to get Alzheimer's and remembers nothing anyway!" Daadima says with frustration.

I stare at her stopped wristwatch and think of all the things that it metaphorically stood for. She picks a piece of her favourite chakli from her plate.

"Do you know that here you're only served the food that you've tried when you were alive? I never tasted that Sizzler we were supposed to go for. And now, I never can," she sighs.

"Damn, really? I always wanted to eat real Japanese sushi!" I lament.

"You eat meat now?" she probes.

Oh no. To avoid answering, I pretend to be distracted by the rainbow.

"There's no rainbow without a storm, beta. If you go back, you'll surely have tough days. But you'll also have magical ones. Let your heart break. Then rebuild it. Lose. And then win. Go to Japan. Eat that sushi. But most importantly, go back and change your last words. Because once that watch stops, everything freezes forever. Time, memories, even regrets"

I sit, numb. In the distance, I hear the humming of hospital machines. Beep... Beep...

"You don't have much time to decide. But know this, I'm here waiting for you today. I'll be here even after forty years. The passage of time is the privilege of the living"

Beep. Beep. It's getting louder. More urgent.

"But... but... I am exhausted all the time! (Beep!) Some days I am completely overwhelmed! (Beep!) I feel no one cares about me (Beep!) That nothing that I will do will ever be enough!" I urgently

make my argument.

Beep. Beep.

"All you have to remember is that..."

BEEEEEP!

I jerk awake. But not before I hear the echoes of her last words to me. *"It'll pass!"*

I am immediately hit by the pungent smell of the hospital disinfectant that has replaced the fragrance of jasmine. Stale air-conditioned air has taken the place of a fresh breeze. The familiar faces of my family are gone. In their place, I see those of relieved doctors. If they came with a thought bubble, it would read *"What just happened?"*

None of this seems like an upgrade. Except that it is. I had upgraded to life from death. I had chosen life over death.

I feel just one all-consuming emotion. Gratitude. For everything that I had and almost lost. I was thrilled at the possibility of seeing my husband and children. I hope they had made good use of their time by throwing themselves at God's feet, showering Him with coconuts and tall promises. Maybe Jay even pleaded, *"God, please let her live! I'll fix everything, including that leaky tap that I should've repaired three months ago!"*

I had chosen chaos, taxes and traffic. And I can't believe that I am saying this, I couldn't wait to get back to the gift of it all.

I must be feeling emotional because I can feel a tear slide from my eye.

"Does it hurt?" the doctor asks.

I wonder how he expects me to answer with a breathing mask on my face. So I nod. The pipe digs into my throat, and I want to scream, but all I can eke out is a whimper.

"It'll pass," the doctor reassures me.

As useless as that response is, it strangely calms me down. Because he's right. All the good and bad of life, it'll pass. And that's exactly what makes it special.

I look at the clock on the wall. It reads 17:30.

Nine and a half hours since I had collapsed. A whole life (and death) experienced in the interim.

I think of the beauty of routine that's unfolding right now in the world outside. Children are going to playgrounds. People are swarming railway stations to get back home. Friends catching up over coffee. Couples are lining up at the promenade to catch the sunset.

The time clicks. 17:31.

"The passage of time is the privilege of the living."

I think of Mom and Dad. They're perhaps having their evening tea, trying to keep a semblance of normalcy going while uneasily waiting to hear if their daughter fought for her life. I wonder how many days before I share tea with them again.

I marvel at the messy miracle that's life. And I promise myself to never take it for granted again.

Because.. *it'll pass.*

~

3

Sol Kadhi – Curry for the Soul

~ Manisha Divan

"Mom! Baa is at it again," bellowed my 14-year-old. I rushed in to see my mum fidgeting with the door, trying to open it. I made her sit again. She was angry. She was livid. She was confused!

Such moments are routine in our household now. A year ago, in a similar haze, she had simply walked out of the house, setting off a frantic manhunt. I scoured one direction, asking every face I passed if they'd seen her. My daughters went the opposite way, questioning security guards and passersby. My husband cut short a work meeting and raced home.

Panic doesn't describe what we felt. Fear clamped our throats, and the thought of her alone on the streets – vulnerable, lost – was unbearable. Just when we were about to call the police, a boy from a neighbouring society brought her home. He'd seen her wandering, muttering my younger daughter's name. Recognizing the connection, he led her back. That child, no taller than her shoulder, had unknowingly returned life to us that day. God bless him.

'Time and tides wait for none' – it's not just a saying – it's a harsh truth I live with daily.

My mother was once one of the fiercest women I knew. Widowed young, she raised four of us with a quiet strength and relentless spirit. She went from homemaker to breadwinner overnight, never once flinching. She was our warrior, our lighthouse. Neighbours revered her. Children adored her. She became the go-to for everything – from school admissions to stormy advice sessions over chai.

Fast forward twenty-five years, and I now find myself holding up a mirror to a stranger. She is here, but only in body. Her presence, once radiant, is now dimmed, flickering like the last embers of a fire refusing to go out.

It started with small forgetfulness: dishes left on the stove, keys in the fridge, questions repeated twice. We brushed it off as age. But soon the lapses deepened – names, places, faces, and eventually, her very sense of self began to crumble. She wandered, sometimes didn't eat for days, mistook the television for a window, or asked for her long-dead brother.

Alzheimer's is a cruel beast. It doesn't just take memories; it takes identity. It strips away dignity in whispers – silent, slow, merciless.

And yet, in rare moments, a flicker breaks through. Like the other day, when I made her favourite: sol kadhi. The aroma of kokum and coconut wafted through the house, and for a heartbeat, I saw something stir in her eyes. I offered her a sip. She closed her eyes, savoured it, and softly said, "Tangy... just right."

Then, as if from the mist, she whispered my name.

"Munna."

It was the first time she had said it in months. My heart clenched, and I knelt by her side, clutching her frail hand. "Yes, Mum. I'm here."

That moment stayed with me for days, replaying like an old record. One word. That was all I needed.

The thing about caring for someone with dementia is that the loss is ongoing. It's not one heartbreak, but a thousand little ones – a daily mourning of what once was.

And yet, amidst the ache, there are moments of quiet beauty.

My younger daughter often sits beside her Baa, brushing her hair, feeding her little spoonfuls of rice, whispering stories from her day at school. "She listens with her heart," she once told me, "even if her ears forget."

It's true. Mum smiles sometimes at the oddest things – a shadow on the wall, a line in a bhajan, the sound of temple bells from afar. It's like her soul still remembers, even when her mind doesn't.

She has now developed a fascination with mirrors. Sometimes she gazes into them, puzzled, sometimes afraid. Once she pointed at her reflection and asked me who the lady was.

I simply said, "Someone who loves you very much."

We've tried everything: medication, dietary changes, pranayama, memory games, chanting. Some of it helped. Most of it just slowed the inevitable. But what truly helps – what truly seems to ground her – is routine, calm, and above all, love.

I've learned to find comfort in the small things. In the way she still folds her dupatta like she did 40 years ago. In the way her hand automatically moves to adjust her bindi even when there's none. In the softness of her voice when she sings old lullabies in fragments.

She may not know my name, but she feels my presence. That's enough.

One evening, I found her on the balcony, standing silently, looking at the sky turn orange. I joined her, and we stood like that for a while.

Then she spoke, very softly. "The birds are going home."

"Yes," I replied, surprised at the coherence.

She turned to me and said, "Where is my home, Munna?"

My throat closed up. What do you say to that?

I gently placed my arm around her and said, "You're home, Mum. You've always been home."

She leaned into me, rested her head on my shoulder like she used to do when I was a child afraid of storms.

My siblings visit when they can. They help in bits, but the daily caregiving is on me. It's exhausting. There are days I break down behind closed doors. But I've never wished it away. This journey – painful as it is – is a chance to serve the woman who once served the world.

Now and then, I cook her favourites – simple things she once made for us with love and warmth: patra, muthiya, theplas, and godpapdi. Food, I've learned, is a bridge. She may forget names and dates, but the warmth of those flavours stirs something ancient in her. Something primal.

Sol kadhi, especially, brings a peace I can't explain. Maybe it's the soothing colour, or the memory of summer afternoons under the fan, her laughter echoing down the hallway. When I serve it to her, it feels like I'm offering her a piece of herself.

I often wonder what she thinks in her quiet moments.

Does she feel lost, or does her mind conjure a parallel world – a place where she's still whole, still the commanding matriarch of our little universe?

There's a strange grace in the way she sits now, her posture calm, her gaze distant, almost meditative, as if she's begun to make peace with the unraveling.

And perhaps, I must too.

Not by giving up, but by surrendering to the present.

She is still with us. She is still alive. Still here to hold, to feed, to tuck in every night. She still hums old Hindi songs. She still responds to temple bells. She still enjoys the softness of a cotton saree on her skin.

I've learned to love her not as she was, but as she is.

A soul still shimmering, despite the fading.

One day, as I brushed her hair before bedtime, she looked at me and said, "I don't remember who you are, but I know you're mine."

That was all I needed.

Time and tides wait for none. But in this space – this now – I have her. And she has me.

And until the tides finally pull her gently away to a place beyond memory, I will be here, holding the fort, making her sol kadhi, brushing her hair, being her home.

~

4

Stained with Turmeric and Time

~ Avani Shah

At first glance, it looked like nothing more than a worn-out journal – dog-eared pages, corners curling with age, and the spine barely holding together. But to me, it is a vessel of time. A storybook not of fables or fiction, but of family and the tide of memory that carried us through generations.

It began, as many stories do, in a kitchen.

As a young girl, sitting cross-legged on the cool stone floor, I would watch the dance of hands and spices orchestrated by my grandmother. The kitchen was her stage. Early on, I realized the transformative power of food in my family. While I was mildly disappointed at not having photographs of my forefathers, the stories of food, people, and places brought them vividly to life. These stories, narrated by my grandmother mid-recipe, in between the laughter and sounds of cumin crackling in hot oil, were as flavourful as the meals she prepared.

"Every spice has a past," she would say, her bangles clinking as she stirred. "And every dish, a memory."

Those early days felt timeless, though I now know time was moving along swiftly.

My grandmother had travelled across borders, forced to leave her home in Karachi during partition. She arrived in India not with possessions, but with recipes – intangible heirlooms passed from her mother's hands to hers. Khajoor pak, sweet date rolls cooked slowly over an open flame, became a symbol of winters that once were, of festivals celebrated, of neighbours now separated by borders but remembered through flavour.

She showed me that food could carry not just the weight of history, but also its lightness. She would smile when she recounted how her Muslim neighbour had taught her to make *Khajoor Pak,* or how her wedding feast was cooked entirely over a wood fire, since there was no gas.

To preserve these moments, I started writing them down – at first in fragments: a measurement here, a story there. But the more I wrote, the more I understood that this wasn't a cookbook. It was a chronicle.

I would document the flavours that defined our celebrations: *Til laddoos* during kite-flying season, rose syrup falooda in the heat of summer, and rice pudding slow-cooked through winter nights. I scribbled notes not just about the ingredients, but also the stories that flowed as freely as the tea. The more she shared, the more I realised that many of our everyday meals had been inspired by the culture we were unacquainted with.

Each dish was a portal to the past.

Seasons changed, years turned, and life moved on. What began in my teenage summer, unknowingly, became the foundation for something far more meaningful. Eventually, my grandmother's voice faded, but others rose to fill the space she left.

The silence in the kitchen after her passing was deafening.

It wasn't just the quiet; it was the absence of the rhythmic clink of her bangles as she kneaded dough, the faint scent of cardamom that always clung to her saris, and her soft hum while stirring a pot.

Her absence lingered not only in empty plates but in the silence between the stirs. For months, I couldn't touch the journal. It felt too heavy, too final.

But grief has its own rhythm. One evening, I opened the journal again. Her handwriting stared back at me – small, neat, precise. In the margins of a dal khichdi recipe, she had written: "Add more curry leaves if you're sad."

I smiled through my tears.

And then, as I began to cook, it dawned on me that she would live on, through us cooking the most delicious food with the simplest recipes. I felt more compelled to complete the work I had begun. I began reaching out to distant relatives, hoping to rekindle old bonds and draw our wider family closer. Initial hesitation gave way to candid conversations, new learnings, and an awareness not just of a shared past, but also of a possible shared future. What began as a quiet project exploded into a full-blown family movement. WhatsApp groups buzzed with recipes and audio recordings of family elders explaining the exact proportions of our family's signature garam masala.

Relatives abroad added new twists to our recipes. One cousin shared his version of our grandmother's dal, reinvented in London with split peas and thyme. Another sent me her twist on rose cheesecake, an accidental Diwali fusion that became an instant hit. From across the globe, family members shared photos and paragraphs, helping me weave a culinary map of our diaspora.

It was astonishing to see the same recipes shift across time zones and tastes, some fiercely spicy, others mellowed, some embracing quinoa, others holding fast to tradition. But at the heart of each dish remained its story: who first made it, when it graced the table, and the meaning it held. And slowly, the tide of time, which once felt cruel, began to feel generous.

The journal had grown thick and lively; its pages full not only of dishes but with personal messages and stories from the past as a preface. Some poignant. Some joyous. Some as spicy as the food itself.

I converted it into a digital book for easier sharing, but the original – the one stained with turmeric, smudged with flour, and marked with fingerprints is the one I treasure the most. It's not perfect, but it is real. Alive.

And the last few pages? They remain blank.

I leave them so for the stories yet to come, for the meals we haven't cooked yet, and for the recipes waiting to be written.

Time, like the tide, takes and gives.

It took my grandmother's voice, but it gave me her stories. It swept away moments I didn't hold tightly enough, but offered back meaning in the memories I chose to preserve.

Through this journal, I've come to believe something deeply: that stories, like recipes, don't fade if we keep cooking them. If we keep telling them. If we pass them down, one dish, one memory at a time.

And so, our story continues – stirred gently, served generously, always seasoned with memory.

~

5

Time, Tide & Tapan

~ Manika Tibriwal

In the laid-back coastal town of Chinchpokli, where the coconut trees danced to the tune of sea breeze gossip and the dogs napped through traffic, lived a man who had constructed his entire life around a single, unshakeable principle: Time was optional. His name? Tapan Biswas.

Now, Tapan wasn't a criminal or even irresponsible; he was simply pathologically tardy. Late to school, late to college, late to weddings, including his own, which never quite happened because he triumphantly arrived after the bride had changed her mind. Legend held that he had even been late to being born – his mother famously described her labour as "a Netflix show that dragged on for 15 seasons too many."

The townsfolk knew him well. If you ever asked, "What time will the function begin?" the answer typically would be, "Not sure, but expect Tapan 45 minutes after." Yet Tapan took this not as an insult, but as a compliment. He believed punctuality was an overrated obsession of the modern world. "Life isn't a train station," he'd say. "It's a beach. Waves don't ask for permission."

The last time Tapan was on time was when he accidentally attended his neighbour's wedding while thinking it was his cousin's funeral. His life was a comedy of errors, and the best part? He was the star in his own show.

As the sand glimmered under the sun, the town meticulously prepared for its most awaited event – the Grand Boat Festival. This festival was the crown jewel, a beloved tradition where fishermen raced their boats at dawn while the townspeople rallied from the shore, drums booming and grandmothers gossiping louder than the waves. In preparation for its centenary edition, the mayor, a rotund man who resembled a guava in suspenders, held a press conference as if it were a UN summit.

"We shall gather at 5:30 A.M. sharp on the beach! The sacred boat race will begin at 5:45 A.M. No excuses, no delays, and particularly no Tapans!" he declared, provoking laughter from the crowd, even the seagulls seemed to caw in agreement.

From his shady spot, Tapan, munching on raw mango with chili powder, grinned and shouted, "This year, I'll be there before the boats are even in the water!" The mayor simply grunted, muttering, "You'll probably show up after the fish go home." However, determination fueled Tapan as he set an alarm for 5:00 A.M., laid out his clothes, and even pre-peeled his coconut to save time.

The morning arrived, a gentle pink hue creeping into the sky as the sun prepared for its grand entrance. The waves hummed like monks in meditation, and the beach buzzed with anticipation. Families adorned in colorful saris and lungis arrived, children clutching conch shells, and vendors hawking puffed rice in newspaper cones. Even Uncle Ramesh, who hadn't walked more than ten steps since 2004, glided in his motorised wheelchair.

But where was Tapan, the town's notorious time-skipper?

He was, in fact, at home... dreaming. In his dream, he stood on a golden boat, sailing into the sunset, with villagers chanting his name. "Tapan! Tapan the Timely!" But in reality, his alarm had vibrated off the table and lodged itself under the bed, flashing vainly like a lost light bulb.

At 6:30 A.M., Tapan ambled onto the beach, sporting sunglasses, a vibrant orange lungi, a folding chair in hand, and an unshakable look of confidence. However, to his shock, the beach was devoid of any life. The boats? Long gone. The tide? Receded. In place of the bustling crowd stood a solitary crab and a bewildered parrot munching on a banana peel.

A little girl poked her mother and asked, "Maa, is that the man who always misses everything?" With a heavy sigh, her mother replied, "Yes, beta. He's the reason we say, 'Time and tide wait for none – especially not Tapan.'" Tapan, unfazed, plopped down on a soggy sand patch, dipped his feet in a leftover puddle, took a sip of his coconut, and boldly declared, "Perfect timing!"

Just then, as if the sea had heard and could no longer tolerate his nonsense, it released a rogue wave that splashed him squarely in the face. SPLASH! Crabs clapped, the parrot chuckled, and the puddle seemed to whisper, "Deserved."

Humiliated but still shameless, Tapan trudged home, soaking wet and his pride in tatters. But halfway back, a realization struck him. "Maybe I'm not actually bad at time... Perhaps I've just been applying it to the wrong profession!" With that thought, he hatched a plan combining his love for food, his longing for vengeance against society, and a newfound motivation to finally be on time.

His target? Papa Pepperoni's Pizza Parlour. A new franchise in town, infamous for its Triple Cheese Rocket Pizza and 24-layer lasagna – both of which Tapan could never afford on his coconut-breaking income.

The plan was bold: rob the parlour late at night, using timing as his ace. For once in his life, Tapan was determined to be early for something.

Immediately, he began surveillance. Disguised as a mop salesman, Tapan paid daily visits to the parlour for "research." He diligently noted the Cleaner left at 10:00 P.M., the Cashier closed the till at 10:15 P.M., and the Security Guard arrived at 10:30 P.M., promptly drifting off to sleep by 10:40 P.M. after indulging in leftover garlic bread.

The operation was set for 10:36 P.M., during that sleepy window. He even recruited one assistant: his pet mouse, Jerry, a sharp-eyed rodent who had once escaped a glue trap using nothing but a pencil and salt. Together, they trained in stealth missions, refining their skills – Jerry learned how to carry keys while Tapan struggled manfully not to wheeze as they practiced their maneuvers.

They drew maps, established signals, and rehearsed their roles, employing cheese slices as currency. The stage was set.

Little did Tapan know, however, that Jerry had a secret: he was in cahoots with Tom, the parlour's resident kitchen cat. An enormous orange creature with the personality of a grumpy waiter and reflexes of a ninja on an energy drink, Tom and Jerry were not enemies but business partners. Their ongoing deal? Jerry distracts, Tom naps, and both receive unlimited pizza crusts from the leftover tray.

However, on this fateful night, Jerry found himself torn between loyalty to his human and a love for free anchovies.

At 10:36 P.M., Tapan tiptoed into the parlour clad in an all-black outfit that included a turtleneck (in coastal humidity), socks with slippers (don't ask), and a belt made from old headphone wires. While Jerry scuttled ahead, ready to unlock the supply cabinet, disaster struck: "MEOW!"

Tom erupted from the freezer with all the enthusiasm of a furry missile. Jerry dropped the keys and froze in panic, and Tom tackled him, compellingly looking at Tapan before triggering the security alarm by stepping on the sauce pedal.

BEEP-BEEP-BEEP! Red lights flashed, sirens blared, and the automatic pepperoni slicer began spinning. As panic set in, Tapan ran straight into the dough roller, flipped over a parmesan bucket, slipped on a tomato, and cascaded across the floor like a mozzarella-filled tumbleweed. He attempted to regain his balance, only to topple into a stack of garlic bread, which erupted around him in an avalanche.

The CCTV, meanwhile, captured the entire fiasco. Tom and Jerry? They were calmly perched on the counter, sipping cold soda and munching on cheese fries, treating it like their own private movie night.

The townsfolk awoke the next day to find the headlines screaming: "TIME-CHALLENGED MAN GETS BAKED: PIZZA FAIL GOES VIRAL!" Tom and Jerry morphed into local heroes, prompting the pizzeria to rename their combo meal: "Tom n Jerry Double Trouble Meal – Comes with a Side of Shame!"

Tapan was sentenced to 30 days of community service, beginning at 5:00 A.M. sharp, for cleaning beaches, peeling garlic, and folding pizza boxes. Shockingly, that turned out to be a transformative experience.

For the first time in his life, Tapan was forced to wake up before dawn. There were no shortcuts or "5 more minutes," just salt on his skin, sweat on his brow, and time discipline introduced by the universe itself. To everyone's surprise, he showed up on time every single day.

Even the seagulls started depending on him. Tapan began folding pizza boxes with exceptional precision, sweeping the beach like a Zen monk with obsession. He even started timing his steps to a metronome! The townspeople noticed him and, at first, they mocked him. Then, they nodded. Finally, smiles began to appear: "Tapan, on time? Next, the fish will vote!"

But it was real, something had shifted within him.

A year later, Tapan opened his own café by the ocean, aptly named "Tapan's Timely Tiffins & Pizza Rolls." His slogan? "On Time. Every Time. Or You Get a Free Coconut." Tapan had transformed his life; he hired staff, he tracked clocks, he colour-coded schedules, and passionately delivered motivational speeches at schools titled "Tick-Tock Tales: How a Pizza Changed My Life."

Unbeknownst to them, the crabs still clapped for him. The mayor even offered him an honorary medal for "Personal Time Reform and Pizza Recovery."

Tom and Jerry would occasionally visit, still smug and still the best of friends, enjoying VIP status in a corner booth dubbed "The Cheese Throne."

And at dawn every morning, Tapan would walk to the beach, gaze out at the sea, and softly whisper, "Thanks for waiting. This time, I'm here."

Life was unpredictable and humorous, a timeless comedy shaped by tides, laughter, and a man named Tapan.

~

6

Secrets of the Sand

~ Yūgen

I was twelve when the wind first called my name.

It wasn't a gust, nor a storm, but a whisper, a quiet breath that curled beneath the eaves of our mud-walled home in Khuri, a sun-scorched village pressed gently into the edge of the Thar Desert. I remember it clearly, for the wind did not just stir the grains on the floor - it stirred something older, something that had long been sleeping inside me.

"Rana."

That's what it said – my name, as if it belonged not just to me, but to the desert itself.

I paused mid-step beside the brass water pot. The air shimmered. I was not afraid, not quite. Just alert, as though my body had remembered something my mind had yet to learn. Even now, decades later, that moment returns to me; not as a memory, but like an unfinished sentence in a language only the wind speaks.

My family lived simply. My father wove jute ropes in the courtyard, his fingers strong and sure. My mother coaxed marigolds to bloom in clay pots, singing old bhajans to them as if they were her children. My sister, barefoot and brown-eyed, fed our goats lullabies. We had no clocks. Time moved with the shadows, warmed by sand, cooled by the scent of rain that never quite came.

But that summer, time began to loosen. It did not pass; it lingered.

As a child, I was curious about strange things. I once spent three days watching ants rebuild their broken trail, charting their path with broken chalk. I sat beside the well and asked questions into its belly. "Where does your darkness go during the day?" I believed the desert held secrets, not in its dunes, but in the pauses between them.

One evening, just as the sun was dipping behind the dunes and the sky turned the colour of ripe apricots, I wandered to the edge of the village and saw a man. An old man, tall and thin as a stick of incense, was tying something to a low-hanging branch of a Khejri tree. He turned, and in the fading light, his eyes caught mine; glassy, pale, and endless.

"You look like a boy who remembers," he said.

He pressed a postcard into my hand. The edges were frayed, the image on it blurred with age – a lake under moonlight, a ripple frozen in silver.

On the back, written in a delicate slant, was:

When you find me, you will find peace.

And beneath it, a name – *Lakhan Bheel.*

"Keep it safe," the old man said. "It's not for now."

And before I could ask him who he was or what he meant, he walked into the dunes. Just like that. The sky swallowed him.

I hid the postcard in a clay jar in the attic, wrapped in a scrap of old muslin. But that monsoon, fierce and moody, rattled our roof. A gust toppled the jar. The card slipped through a crack in the wall. Gone. I dug; I begged the bricks to give it back. I even lit incense and whispered into the chisel marks. But the wall remained silent.

Years passed. I grew, left Khuri, and tried to become someone new. I found work repairing radios, then computers, and after a while, people's broken silences too. I thought I was building something – a business, a name, a life – but all it took was one hard year for the scaffolding to collapse. The business I started grew too fast, then failed in ways I hadn't prepared for. My friends grew distant, one by one. My wife and I stopped talking. Then she left. And the silence that remained wasn't the kind I could fix.

The city, which once lit up like a field of stars, grew dim and loud and heavy.

Everything I built turned unfamiliar. I felt like a guest in my own story.

So, I returned to Khuri, not as a man with answers, but one looking for a place to fall apart quietly.

Our house stood like a paused breath. The marigolds were gone, but the neem tree waited. I climbed to the attic, heart full of dust. As I reached for an old box, my fingers brushed a crack in the wall – that same old crack – and something thin, familiar, paper-soft slid into my hand.

The postcard.

Unfaded. Unspoiled. As if no time had touched it.

When you find me, you will find peace.

I held it like a heartbeat.

Lakhan Bheel.

It meant nothing. And yet, I asked. I asked the grocer, the priest, and a child carrying an aluminium pot. Names live long in villages. Someone remembered.

He lived near the temple well – a man with one eye lost to time, the other sharp as a kite's. He looked at me, and in his gaze, I saw the boy I once was.

"You're late," he said simply.

He handed me a small iron box, old but intact. Inside were gold bangles, a nose ring, and bundles of currency. On top, a folded note:

For the boy who listens to the wind, from Thakurji's granddaughter.

It belonged to my great-grandmother.

I sat awake the entire night, the wind nudging the curtain like a cat wanting in. By morning, the answer had shaped itself.

I used the money to open a centre, not a business, but a space. For girls to learn without fear. For elders to teach without being forgotten. For travellers to rest and leave stories behind. We named it Vayu Bhavan – the House of the Wind.

It wasn't easy. Villagers were sceptical at first. They whispered – who was this man returning empty-handed, carrying only shadows and failed city dreams? But slowly, something shifted. I built with my own hands, brick by hopeful brick. I invited the potter's daughter to teach clay art. I asked a retired schoolmaster to read stories under the banyan tree. I planted marigolds outside the gates.

Girls came first, then grandmothers. We offered classes in reading, stitching, computers, and sometimes, just listening. On Thursdays, we served halwa and chai. On Sundays, travelling musicians played songs older than memory.

And people came.

Curious at first, then hopeful. Journalists wrote about it. Donors offered funds. City folk called me visionary. But I knew better. I had not built it. I had only listened.

Today, I sit beneath the neem again, the same wind playing with my shawl. A boy, about twelve, lingers nearby.

"What are you listening to, uncle?"

I smile.

"The wind," I say. "It remembers things we forget."

He watches me a moment longer, then runs off. The breeze nudges the postcard still folded in my lap.

Because some messages are not meant for mailboxes. Some arrive before their time, and wait; in attic cracks, in whispers, in wind.

Waiting, perhaps, for someone like him.

Just as it once waited for me.

~

7

Reclamation

~ Madhuja Banerjee

It was raining outside.

Sitting on an old wooden chair, Shoma was trying to manage the excruciating pain twisting through her stomach. She felt nauseated. She considered going back to the hotel room, but that wasn't an option. Ribhu was inside, taking his English exam – the final step in his admission test.

What would happen if he finished early and came out to find his mother wasn't there? The little eight-year-old had never been to Mumbai before. He had chosen to follow her here because he trusted her.

Trust.

The word was beginning to fade for Shoma. Yet, when she looked at her son, she rediscovered it.

The nausea was rising again. She felt as if she might collapse any moment. But she couldn't afford to – not now. If Ribhu saw her in that state, he would panic.

Glancing at her phone, she decided to switch it off.

The first message had come from Suchi:

"Have you seen today's Page 3?"

Shoma replied, *"No – I'm not in Kolkata. What happened? Any story we missed?"*

Shoma, a senior Page 3 journalist at a leading Kolkata newspaper, usually began her day with the news. Highly competitive in her field, she hated missing anything. She was always the first to break Tinseltown scoops. The Bengali film industry was like a small island – it wasn't hard to get news if you knew where to look.

But Suchi's message made her pause. Something didn't feel right.

Then again, that wasn't her priority now. Her transfer request to Mumbai had already been approved. She was house-hunting and trying to find the right school for Ribhu.

Kolkata wasn't as cosmopolitan. At home, they spoke Bangla, and she'd worried if Ribhu could pass the entrance test for a top school. But just a few days before coming to Mumbai, she noticed he had started speaking to her in English. He was trying – just like her – only for one reason: to stay close.

Lost in her thoughts, another message came in. This time, from Aditya.

"Are you free to talk?"

She called him back, assuming he needed help booking an Uber or a train ticket. He never quite got the hang of the digital world.

"Yes, tell me," she said.

"Can you call Katha once?" he asked.

Katha.

The name itself made Shoma sick.

It was because of Katha that Shoma had finally decided to leave Kolkata. Until now, she had always refused transfers, even with promotions. "Family comes first," she would tell her bosses, proud of the image they projected: a power couple.

Aditya, a budding film director with two back-to-back hits, chased his silver screen dreams. Shoma, juggling work and home, had become a role model in her newsroom. She felt fulfilled. For a while.

That feeling was now broken.

She had sensed it – the quiet shift. She never voiced her suspicions about Aditya's growing closeness with Katha. As a matter of fact, Katha had been her discovery. She met her backstage at a fashion show, saw potential in her, and encouraged her to model. She'd even recommended her to Aditya.

Katha made her debut in one of his films. Awards followed. So did attention.

An affair between a mentor and protégé was nothing new. The sudden intimacy had made Shoma uneasy, but she had silenced her thoughts. She didn't want to question Aditya's integrity – or the trust in their relationship.

But denial has a shelf life.

She began to feel embarrassed when photographers showed her party pictures of Aditya and Katha, while she was buried in editorial deadlines or helping Ribhu with exams. The final blow came when Aditya's friends began cracking jokes – nasty ones.

Her safe little cocoon cracked. Still, she couldn't bring herself to confront him.

She knew exactly what he'd say:

"Arre, this is all bullshit. You know how our profession is. Why are you even worried?"

But she was worried.

Fifteen years of marriage had taught her that intimacy fades. But she still longed for his touch. She couldn't even remember the last time he'd kissed her on the cheek.

She realized she didn't feel jealous of Katha anymore – just disappointed in Aditya. She couldn't think of divorce, but she couldn't keep living in denial either.

Her only hope was Mumbai.

She liked this city. She knew its rhythm. Mumbai was indifferent – but in that indifference, one could rediscover oneself.

At forty, stepping out of her comfort zone was difficult. But it wasn't harder than silently watching her husband's open affair.

She was intelligent. Independent. And, most importantly, brave.

She would fight back.

And she was grateful Ribhu had agreed to come with her.

After a long pause, snapping out of her reverie, Shoma asked Aditya, "Why?"

"Just do me a little favour. Please call Katha once. She's extremely upset," he said.

"But why me?"

"Everything happened just because of you."

"What happened? I don't understand."

"Check WhatsApp – I'm forwarding you something."

Shoma opened the app.

A deep silence gripped her.

The classroom hallway was still and cold. She could hear her heartbeat, could feel the breath catch in her chest.

A rival newspaper had published a story featuring Aditya. The headline read:

"New Love in Aditya's Life"

There was a photo of Katha brushing a strand of hair from Aditya's shoulder. The piece listed every event, every sighting, reconstructed like a timeline.

For the first time, Shoma wasn't lamenting a missed scoop.

She was burning with public humiliation.

"Why should I call Katha?" she asked calmly.

"She's deeply upset. And I'm sure I've been framed – because of you," he said.

"Me? How can you link me to this?"

"You need to understand, Shoma. Your rivals are jealous of your success. They've made us scapegoats. Please say sorry to Katha."

Shoma paused.

She stared at the screen again. The photo. The headline. The sly captions. Every word screamed mockery. Not at Aditya.

At her.

When she finally spoke, her voice was even. Measured. Unshaken.

"Aditya," she said. "I won't call her."

"What? But – "

"I'm not responsible for your choices or your consequences. You wanted to play the game. Now play it."

"Shoma, please – don't let your ego – "

"This isn't ego. Its boundaries. Something I should've drawn years ago."

She hung up.

Her hands trembled, but she felt an unexpected clarity. Not rage – resolve.

She wiped her damp palms on her kurta and checked the time. Ten minutes until Ribhu's exam ended. Her body tensed again.

What if he didn't do well?

What if this whole move had been a mistake?

She had uprooted everything for this boy. Because he trusted her. Because he chose her. Because he didn't even ask to stay with his father.

A sharp knock broke her thoughts.

A small figure appeared in the doorway – Ribhu, clutching a folded slip of paper. His eyes scanned the hallway until they met hers. A grin spread across his face.

"Ma! I got selected! They said I can join next month!" he shouted, breathless.

Shoma blinked. "What? Really?"

He nodded eagerly, eyes sparkling. "They said I was very good in English and I can join Class Four directly!"

Shoma crouched and hugged him tightly, hiding her tears in his damp shirt.

In that moment, her pain, her nausea, her anger, blurred into the background.

Her son had found a place in this city.

And maybe – just maybe – so could she.

—

As the taxi moved through the puddled lanes and honking streets of Juhu, Shoma looked out at the city she once knew only as a correspondent.

Now, it will be home.

She remembered reading that Mumbai was once a cluster of seven scattered islands – vulnerable and isolated. Over the years, it was reclaimed from the sea, stitched together through effort and persistence until it became one city.

That fact stayed with her, not just as geography, but as a metaphor.

Reclamation. Reinvention.

Mumbai wasn't built in a day. And neither would she be.

But perhaps it was time for her, too, to reclaim and redevelop.

She smiled – soft, faint, but real.

She would rebuild herself. Not by erasing the past, but by reclaiming it – her identity, her pride, her voice.

She would no longer be a footnote in Aditya's story.

She would begin writing her own.

There was still a lot to do – find Ribhu's school uniform, fix the leaky kitchen tap, sort out groceries for the week.

But beneath those ordinary tasks ran something extraordinary:

A quiet, returning strength.

She caught her reflection in the rearview mirror. Her eyes looked tired, but steady.

Mumbai wasn't waiting to welcome her. It never did that for anyone.

But that was the beauty of it. In a city built on reclamation, Shoma would find her space.

~

8

The Last Catch

~ Archana Maru Nanda

It was 7.30 pm, and Rudra's mother, Devika, settled him in her arms before opening his Environmental Studies book and reading through his answers. She noticed his responses were meticulous, and his interest in the subject was evident. Water Pollution was the next chapter in the text, and Devika asked if he wanted to hear a story about it. Rudra nodded, wiggled, and nestled in even more comfortably, cocking his ear.

Devika thought for a moment and began her story about a *Koli* (fisherman) named Chandrakant.

Chandrakant lived in a humble cave house with wooden doors that opened onto the sea. He would wake early every day, well before sunrise, when the sky was still a bruised purple. When he slept, the inky sky filled with constellations, the moon reflected in the sea, and the waves would swell up to talk to the moon and fall back again in a rhythmic dance all night. The comforting smell of the sea, the salty air, and a deep, inexplicable connection with the water and tides made Chandrakant calm and content.

His father and grandfather had taught him how to read the sea. They could tell by the colour of the water and the angle of the wind where the fish would congregate. When the tide moved from high to low, it was time to take out the boat and bring in a catch to sell in the market. It was almost twenty years ago that he first went out with his father early one morning. The sea was alive with a silvery mass of fish, providing them with both livelihood and food. On a miraculous day, one fisherman caught over 150 croakers in his net, making him an overnight millionaire.

"The sea is kind to us," his father would say. "We must always be grateful and look after it."

But the passage of time wilted the wealth the sea had once freely shared with all who came to her. Today, Chandrakant's net wrestled with plastic and metal instead of the kindness of the sea. He would often come back after a whole morning with just a few skinny mackerels, some sardines, confused crabs, and a pomfret if he was lucky. The buyers at the local market would not haggle for this.

His friend Amar was at the pier one morning, staring at his own empty nets.

"I sold my nets yesterday," he told Chandrakant. "I've got a job as a security guard. The black water from the new chemical factory will kill us all. There's nothing left to catch."

Rudra stirred a little, digesting the image of pollution. Devika paused.

"What will Chandrakant do now?" he asked.

Chandrakant's days blended into a long struggle. He came home with disappointment and little else. At the market, the buyers were unhappy with the fish, threatening to move to the next village, even if it cost more.

One day, he made a brave decision. If he was not able to fill his fishing nets that day, he would sell his boat.

He rowed further out into the incoming tide. It was his last chance. He stayed out all day until the sun sank into the horizon. The water had an oily slick, and the sea felt lifeless. Chandrakant paddled home silently with his small catch and sat on the rocks outside his door.

"Then what, Mamma? What happened to him?" asked Rudra, a little sleepy now.

"Well, Rudra," said Devika, "fishing is one of the oldest professions in the world, and it's hard to leave after so many generations have worked in the same way. But listen to what happens. There was hope."

Chandrakant heard a woman's voice behind him.

"Are you going to sit there all night?"

He turned to see a young and confident-looking woman with clean shoes and a bright jacket.

"Hi. I'm Mira. I'm a marine biologist and work with Ocean Restore. We test water quality and build gardens to reduce toxic matter. Would you care to help?"

"Do I look like a gardener? I'm a fisherman," retorted Chandrakant.

"Really?" replied Mira, glancing at the empty nets.

Something in her tone made Chandrakant emotional, and he looked down at the ground.

The next morning, instead of casting his nets, he ferried bamboo poles, ropes, and barrels for Mira's group. He watched as her team built small floating rafts, covered in plants – water hyacinths, mangroves, even special reeds. Mira explained that these were especially good at absorbing pollution from the sea.

It wasn't fishing, Chandrakant thought. But it was... something. Like the possibility of living on a planet that was also living.

He pulled sacks of garbage from the shore, his arms aching and his hands calloused. At the end of the day, Mira offered him a sandwich and water.

"You really worked the hardest today," she said with a smile.

Chandrakant could not smile back. But something loosened in his chest.

—

Time passed, and weeks became months. Chandrakant kept working with the Ocean Restore group. He learnt aquaponics from Mira – raising small fish and vegetables in tanks, away from the poisoned sea. She showed him seaweed farming, a trade for which buyers in the city paid well. She explained how seaweed could remove carbon dioxide from the water and provide nutrients for fish and sea life.

His boat, once nearly sold for nothing, became his new best friend. He ferried seedlings, built rafts, and harvested strands of emerald-green seaweed. His income grew, little by little.

One evening, as the sun dipped into the water, Amar stopped by the dock. He stared at Chandrakant's boat, now loaded with seaweed ropes and fish tanks.

"Are you a farmer now, huh?"

Chandrakant looked at the horizon, where the bay still bore its oily scars.

"No," he said quietly. "Still a fisherman. Just fishing for the future."

The sea hadn't abandoned him. It had simply taught him to change.

—

Three years had passed since Chandrakant first ferried bamboo and seedlings for Mira's team. The bay, once a graveyard, had begun to breathe again.

The floating gardens had spread like a necklace across the water, filtering toxins and giving new homes to crabs and small fish. The seaweed farms thrived, drawing in buyers from across the region.

One morning, Chandrakant cast his net – not out of need, but out of habit. When he pulled it back, it was wriggling with life: small silver anchovies, a couple of mackerels, and a baby crab. Not enough for a market haul, but enough to know the sea was healing.

Mira smiled.

"Told you she would come back," she said, nodding at the sea.

Chandrakant nodded.

"The sea is patient. She needed someone to fight for her."

He felt like a steward of the sea, an eco-warrior with a purpose.

The fishermen of the village, many of whom had partially turned to seaweed farming, gathered around him. That evening, they shared a meal – grilled fish, seaweed chutney, and stew. For the first time in years, amidst the laughter and cheer, Chandrakant could feel a sense of community – but most importantly, an emotional rebirth in his being.

"So, what do you think, Rudra?" Devika asked.

She would have to wait until the next morning. Rudra was fast asleep, a whisper of a smile on his angelic face.

~

9

Time Will Test You

~ *Dr. Vani Parekh*

Six-year-old Sita found herself standing at the Lahore station. A cloth bag, with whatever little belongings she could collect, in her right hand, her mother's hand clutching her left, and confusion galore in her head. She couldn't understand why they left it all behind. Her red brick house, her cows, her friends, her clothes, her life. Her mother told her they were never going to return, that they had to get on this train anyhow, and get to their mama's, maternal uncle's, home. She looked around her, at the sea of people swarming the station. Was everyone leaving behind their life, the way she was? Why wouldn't they return? With a heavy heart, she hopped on the train with her mother. Her mother prayed the whole journey; she prayed till they reached Delhi station.

It was an arduous journey of twelve hours, followed by another two hours of walking. They finally reached her uncle's house. It was small, nearly half the size of the house she left behind. Her thoughts went to her red brick house. Who must be living in it now? What would've happened to her beloved cows? Just as she was thinking, her cousin Rama came running to see her. They had never met before. She was neatly dressed and appeared confident. Sita hid behind her mother, suddenly self-conscious about her shabby appearance. Her aunt gave them a simple dinner. The atmosphere was sombre.

"You'll have to make do with whatever little we have, I'm afraid. Our house isn't as big as the one you had in Lahore," said her aunt.

"Please don't be silly. We are eternally grateful to you for providing us with a roof over our heads," said her mother.

That night, Sita slept with her mother on a thin chatai on the floor. "Why are we here, mother? Is this our new home? What has happened to everyone in Lahore?"

"Ssshh, my child, we will figure everything out in a while. Time is testing us. But for now, just close your eyes and sleep, and thank our dear lord Krishna that we are alive and healthy."

As she closed her eyes, she went back to her first home, a vision flashed, that red brick house she'd left behind, her cows, her friends, the train, the station platform. Exhaustion took over, and she fell into a deep slumber.

—

Sita was sitting restlessly alone on the balcony. Dressed in a heavy red sharara with gold gotta patti. She could hear the dhol and the loud baraat, inching closer. The last ten years went by, in a blink, or achingly slow, she couldn't tell right now. Her mother worked hard stitching clothes. She had started by going from door to door, to getting a sewing machine, and now finally having their own little shop selling Punjabi suits, awfully inspired by what one would call Lahori designs. They had moved houses three times over the last ten years. And finally, when Sita thought that she had settled down in her new house with a terrace, it was time for her to move again.

Rama came running up the stairs excitedly. She looked as lovely as the pretty bride herself. "They're here", she said.

"Are you ready?" "As ready as I can be, I suppose." What else was she supposed to say? She was getting married to someone she'd never met. Leaving behind everything she knew, once again. Can anyone ever be ready for these moments? Rama held her hand as they walked down the stairs.

She met her mother at the foot of the stairs. She held her hand tight like she always had in the most crucial moments of her life. She looked at her and said, "Time will test you, again and again, but you'll be all right". With those words, her mother took Sita's ghoongat from her head and brought it down, completely covering her face. She walked in slow, small steps to the mandap. As the pandit went on chanting in his slow drawl, her mind drifted somewhere far. Fleeting glimpses of a red brick house, her cows, her friends, the train, the station platform. She sighed. It was time to stand up for the pheras.

—

She always waited at the gate for them, outside their modest house in Chandni Chowk, when they would return from school. Their constant chattering, the scampering of their feet. Baljit was twelve, Ranbir was ten, and they were pieces of her heart. Something was different that day, though. She saw Baljit carrying Ranbir as he limped slowly. She ran towards her boys. She could see that her younger one was holding back tears, trying to keep a brave face as he described to his mother how he got into an accident. She took them inside, examined his knee, applied an ointment, and bandaged his knee.

He rested his head on her lap, and as she stroked his hair, he asked her, "Why did that bike hit me? I was minding my own business, walking where I was supposed to. Why me?"

She asked him to say a silent prayer to their Krishna and thank him that he was alive and well. "Time likes to test us," she said, "but you'll be fine."

—

Standing on the balcony of their posh south Delhi bungalow, she watched her garden from above. She loved the gigantic magnolias at this time of the year. She took pride in her garden. From above, she watched as Baljit sat in his fancy black car, with his wife and their two-year-old. She was a stunningly beautiful baby. As she looked at her granddaughter from the balcony, and marvelled at how wonderful the picture looked in front of her eyes, a series of pictures passed her mind suddenly, a red brick house, her cows, her friends, the train, the station platform. How many years had it been then? How far along had she come? She took a deep sigh, took in the view in front of her, and went back inside.

—

She was lying down on her bed. Her head hurt. Her body wasn't what it used to be. But summer break was on, and her bed was full of loud chattering. Her grandkids just wouldn't stop. What was this accent that they had now? What was with this new body language? They were all teenagers, but in her head, they were little babies. When did they grow up? Where did the time fly? The older two girls were whispering something.

Her ears were still sharp. She caught on to them and asked, "Are you two discussing a heartbreak?" They sheepishly looked at each other, and the younger one chirped in, "Yes, Dadi, Riya got dumped by her boyfriend!" Sita looked and asked, "Dumped? Why would you use a word like that? Your sister's not some garbage that can be dumped."

She held her granddaughter's soft, gentle hands in her rough, wrinkly ones and said, "My darling, there's iron in your blood and steel in your bones. Your great-grandmother was a single mother who crossed the border alone with her daughter. We have lived through the harshest days and survived smiling. This is the blood that runs in you. You're blessed and fortunate that life has been so smooth for you."

But Dadi, she said, "A heartbreak is a heartbreak, and however trivial it may seem to you, it still hurts." She realised the deep truth in her voice, and gave the one advice that she always stood by, "It's all right, my darling, I understand, but always remember, time will test you, but you will be fine."

—

All through the highs and lows, the ups and downs, and at the end of it all, there was peace within her. As she closed her eyes, she went back to her first home, a vision flashed, that red brick house she'd left behind, her cows, her friends, the train, the station platform. She smiled. Whatever test time took, she knew that she did good.

~

10

The Bookmark

~ Monaaz Bamji

"If you ever have a dream in your heart, don't ever let it go..."

Chapter 1

Becky, a spirited young girl, was super excited for her thirteenth birthday! Yes!!! This was the Big Day she had been waiting for! She was now officially a teenager and was on the threshold of turning into a young adult in just a few years. Becky used to envy the freedom her two elder sisters had just because they were a few years older than her. "How unfair!" she complained when her mother reprimanded her for wearing her sister's stilettos and strutting around the house. Time and again, all that she got was a big, "NO!"

NO high heels, NO nail paint, NO hair colour, NO makeup, NO staying up late – it was all a big NO!

"But you're only a child!" explained her mother when Becky protested. Becky had this restless urgency to grow up quickly. So, being a year older was like a step closer to her freedom and her dreams.

It was a bright summer morning, and the warm sun peeped through the large French windows, partially covered by curtains painted with flowers of a violet hue. Even though it was a lazy Sunday morning, Becky jumped out of bed when she realised that she had woken up as a teen that day! She could barely contain her excitement while she stumbled out of bed, nearly knocking over the lampshade by her bedside. The aroma of sweet vermicelli filled the air, and Becky was drawn towards the heady scent like a magnet. When Becky entered the kitchen, her mother was busy whisking the vermicelli, which she had specially prepared for Becky. "Good morning, my love! Happy Birthday!" exclaimed her mother, giving Becky a tight hug. Becky's father came into the kitchen and held out a beautifully wrapped gift in gold paper with a giant rose motif in the centre. Becky was ecstatic and grabbed her gift with both hands. "Thank you!" she exclaimed.

Eager to see the contents of her gift, Becky hurriedly opened the wrapper and found two books by her favourite author. A jubilant glow swept across Becky's face. She was overjoyed!

Becky had been a voracious reader right from her early days and loved getting lost in the imaginary world of books. She dreamed of being a great writer someday and losing herself in the flowing river of words. Amidst the school work that usually buried her, Becky took time out frequently to write essays or poetry and express her beautiful thoughts on paper. However amateur her writing skills were, she still took immense pride in her ability and flair for writing.

When Becky opened the gift wrapper, right on top of the books was a neatly placed bookmark. It read: *"If you ever have a dream in your heart, don't ever let it go..."*

Becky carelessly tossed the bookmark aside and eagerly browsed through the books.

Chapter 2

Becky grew up to be an intelligent adult. Her vast reading developed her interest in various subjects. Her growing understanding of the world made her realise that there was a lot more to adult life than just wearing make-up and stilettos. Her expansive knowledge on different topics made her breeze through college. Soon, she enrolled at a very prestigious business school in the country. All through the years, she cherished her prized possession, her bookmark, like a life companion. One book got replaced by another, but her bookmark remained eternal like a thought frozen in time; although she never quite understood the essence of that line, which always glared back at her: *"If you ever have a dream in your heart, don't ever let it go..."*

In the new town where Becky moved for her higher studies, life unfolded each day with new challenges; a little sweet, a little sour and many times with a bittersweet yearning to scurry back to the familiar abode she called home. This was the first time that Becky was living away from her family; three whole years until her post-graduation. At the same time, there was this euphoric sense of liberation and independence, the onset of a new beginning.

After the initial adjustments, Becky got busy with her preparations for the mid-term exams. With the pressure of studies mounting each day, Becky found it hard to pursue her passion for writing. The looming deadlines for countless project submissions and preparing for the exams simultaneously seemed like the most formidable task she faced. To add to her misery, her roommate Rebecca was a churlish girl with no inclination to study and constantly mocked Becky's anxiety about the exams.

One evening, Rebecca rudely barged into the room, talking into her cell phone at full volume. Her incessant banter made Becky's head spin. As soon as the call was done, Rebecca grabbed Becky's book, completely disregarding her study time and mocked, "You poor creature, you look so burdened! Get a life!"

Becky snapped back, "Well, Rebecca, I am preparing for a great future and will surely do something worthwhile once I am equipped with my degree. And you've got to work hard for it!"

Rebecca scoffed at Becky and said, "Ha! Now don't bore me with your sermons. You are so focused on getting your degree that you are not really aware of what you desire to do eventually!" Rebecca stormed out of the room, leaving Becky bewildered.

Normally, Becky would barely pay heed to Rebecca's nasty comments, but this time it left her pondering. Becky took out her cherished bookmark and stared at it for a while. She was beginning to understand what it meant and mulled over it: *"If you ever have a dream in your heart, don't ever let it go..."*

All of a sudden, the clock struck twelve and jolted Becky back to reality. She had a project submission the next morning and raced to complete it.

As days turned into months, Becky barely got time to pursue her passion for writing, and it eventually waned. Three years sprinted by in a jiffy, and finally, Becky was armed with her degree, beaming with delight.

Chapter 3

Becky set out on a new journey in her life in the corporate world. She demonstrated intelligence, talent and tact and took little time to master her job. Very soon, she rose through the ranks. However, she felt rather unfulfilled in this highly competitive, ruthless struggle to excel at any cost. Mr. Clooney, Becky's boss, was a stout fellow with balding grey hair and unkind eyes. He was generous with throwing his weight around and giving orders to his subordinates, but was a miser when it came to giving any appreciation. He had no compassion for the people around him and took pleasure in making them work until their backs broke. His co-workers passed snide remarks when he passed by and made caricatures of him with devil horns and flaming eyes, spewing venom at them. Nonetheless, they continued to be tormented by him, struggling to stay afloat. Every morning, upon seeing him, they would sigh and secretly wish that a saviour would come and rescue them from his clutches.

In due course, the pressure got the best of Becky, and she finally decided to confront her boss. His lackadaisical attitude made it hard to have a rational conversation with him. Nevertheless, Becky pleaded, "Mr. Clooney, you will appreciate that I have always been a valuable resource for this company. But these gruelling hours and continuous stress are taking a toll on me. I will not be able to continue this way until you either reduce the load or give an extra set of hands!" Mr. Clooney looked up at Becky with an air of arrogance and roared, "Do you think you are obliging me? Next time you complain, think twice, it will only jeopardise your time here!" An astonished Becky walked back to her desk in a daze, highly dejected.

In her quest for success, somewhere along the way, Becky had lost herself, her zeal, her originality. She wondered what the definition of success really meant and whether it was all worthwhile, when in reality, she felt empty inside. Becky glanced at the bookmark, which was pinned to her desk and wondered if this was where she dreamed of landing one day. She was disheartened to realise that after all these years, she had accomplished many goals, but not her dreams. Going back in time, she adored the thirteen-year-old Becky who was so sure of everything and followed her passions fearlessly.

Becky decided that to save herself from the daily anguish, she needed to divert her mind to more meaningful things. She joined a local writer's club and re-ignited her passion for writing. Coincidentally, during one of the informal gatherings of the club, she was surprised to bump into none other than her eccentric roommate, Rebecca! Fifteen long years since they had waved their good-byes; time had revealed to both of them new dimensions of life, making them older and wiser.

"Oh my god! Is that really you? Becky! You look just the same!" Rebecca exclaimed, unable to conceal her excitement.

Becky looked up, startled, trying to recognise the suave, refined and elegant woman in front of her. Her perplexed look made Rebecca chuckle. She gave Becky a quick hug and said, "It's Rebecca, remember?"

Becky gasped in disbelief, "After all these years, Rebecca! You look amazing!"

Rebecca had transformed into this sophisticated, gracious lady, a far cry from the wild child that she had been back in her post-graduation days. Becky felt a warmth in her gestures; something she had never earlier associated Rebecca with. For the first time, she was pleased to run into her.

Rebecca continued, "I know I was a bully back then, but in time I came to realise how it hurts others around me. I was just a bit immature and probably envious of you. You always seemed to be so sure of yourself. Well, better late than never...

I am sorry for being such a pain back then." Becky smiled kindly at Rebecca and said, "That's alright, I always knew you weren't that bad after all. In all these years, I have met some real tyrants, I can assure you that!" And they both burst out laughing.

Becky and Rebecca proceeded towards the delicious snacks, which were laid out artistically in one corner of the room. They could barely wait to catch up on the good old times and the years gone by. Rebecca went on, "After graduation, I made some bad choices and was rather aimless. But fortunately, during one of my temporary jobs, I found a mentor who made me realise my potential. From then on, it's been awesome. As you can see, I am managing this particular event for the writer's club. It sounds crazy, but I always imagined bumping into you at one of these events. I know you were natural at writing. I am glad you followed it through.

Becky replied, "Not really, Rebecca. It's been pretty recently that I joined this club, although I hope to follow my dream now."

After that chance meeting, Becky and Rebecca kept in touch often and in no time, Becky went on to release her first book. From that moment on, there was no looking back. Becky's numerous books received a lot of praise and admiration. But what remained close to her heart through this exhilarating journey of self-discovery was her bookmark that inspired her with the timeless quote: *"If you ever have a dream in your heart, don't ever let it go..."*

~

11

Beyond the Postcard: Escape from Paradise

~ Nily Mehta

November of 1999

Unbelievable! My first solo vacation, and I found myself stranded in one of the world's most breathtaking locations.

Here I was, isolated, praying silently, full of pleas within this old church that was sheltering me from the stormy weather and furious snow outside. The air vibrated with the savage assault of wind and echoes of rain pounding the heavy wooden door and roof. The nearby river's enraged roar mingled with the thunder's deep rumbling, resonating powerfully through the soaring high ceilings of this ancient church.

Time, like a relentless river, continued its flow, utterly indifferent to the turmoil. Within the confines of the church, however, each passing moment stretched into an eternity. My thoughts drifted back, as I reminisced about the genesis of how I landed on this "dream" trip...

—

Six months ago, Mumbai

"...Those were our esteemed runner-up. And now, the moment you've been waiting for: our Grand Winner..." crackled the microphone.

The Swiss tourism board had organized a conference for travel agents in Mumbai, where I lived, to help promote tourism. I was a trainee in a travel company, and I came only because I was the only one in my agency who was excited to learn and meet new people. My other colleagues had done it several times before and found it repetitive.

Never lucky at winning anything, I was already raiding the buffet when they picked out the lucky winner's visiting card. I could have dropped my plate when I heard my name, "Sonia Mehra." I quickly gulped the mouthful of food and raced to the podium.

I received a voucher that said: "Complimentary luxury accommodation in 5-star hotels all over Switzerland and an unlimited First-Class Swiss Rail travel pass for two full weeks!

Wohooo!

—

Stranded! (Temperature below 3° Celsius)

"Don't go near the river". They had explicitly cautioned.

I observed the police and military personnel as I struggled my way uphill, battling the fierce wind. Yet I had no choice. Dwindling funds demanded cheaper lodging. Defying the warnings and the elements, I decided to investigate if the youth hostel on the far side of the river had a vacancy for a solo traveller. Other cheaper options were full, a consequence of the storm prolonging other guests' stays.

Lacking snow boots, each step through the ankle-deep snow was a cold, wet squish; my sneakers were no match for the conditions. The jacket, while thick, couldn't prevent the drenching of the scarf.

I lost my umbrella (it got stolen from the bucket outside the station), so I purchased a new one, but it only offered scant protection against the wild, stormy, windy, and rainy weather. Visibility was poor; it was uphill but navigable. The bridge was seen, yet the river below it surged and raged. Its current intensifying to a wild torrent, sweeping along a dark tapestry of debris and mud along in its powerful flow.

Just then, a thunderous, ear-splitting crash and boom tore through the air, vibrating through the bones, and was unnervingly close. I stood still and frozen, squinting my eyes, then shielded them with my palm, striving to penetrate the gloom and identify the source of the horrific sound. For a moment, only confusion reigned. Then, cold dread:

It was an AVALANCHE!

From midway up the mountain's slopes to the bridge became a scene of horror. A torrent of snow, ice, rocks, uprooted vegetation, and soil plummeted earthward, gathering speed with terrifying momentum. A vast cloud of snow and dust billowed, the roar growing to a deafening rumble as it indiscriminately devoured the landscape.

I panicked and made a desperate attempt to outrun the deluge, in vain. I could only spot a church nearby, offering the only hope of refuge, so I decided to seek shelter there.

—

Coordinates: 46°.02' N, 7°.74' E

Zermatt is a picturesque, car-free village nestled in the Swiss Alps, renowned for its stunning views of the Matterhorn and its excellent skiing and hiking opportunities. The train is the primary mode to reach here, and locally, electric cars can be used to reach popular spots. But in 1999, these were limited, and the frequency changed based on seasons. It was mid-November, and ski lifts, cable cars, electric buggies, and some other services, including many resorts, shut down in the low season.

The majestic and awe-inspiring views of the Matterhorn (at 4478m) in the Alps, it's the pyramid shape that draws the tourists here. It is the highest mountain station in Europe.

My Swiss journey was nearing its conclusion. It had been a grand tour (so far), beginning in Geneva, moving through Lucerne and Interlaken, leading to Zermatt, and finally Zurich. Throughout my experience had been lavish, my stays in the finest hotels and resorts, thanks to the Swiss Tourism Board, I was "so lucky" as others had said enviously.

Arrival the previous morning had been serene, followed by a leisurely day and an early night. It was only at breakfast that the reality struck. An unexpected revelation from the lobby manager: a severe overnight snowstorm had severed Zermatt's connections to the world. The only form of communication channels then: landlines (STD/ISD) and dial-up internet, were all out!

Only then did I look outside to see a pristine, yet isolating, blanket of snow. The gravity of the situation hit when I was informed that all external communication – phones, television, and radio – was cut, and the crucial rail tracks were damaged, preventing any departure until they were fixed!

A cold knot of panic tightened in my stomach. Affording an indefinite stay at this luxurious resort was simply not possible. Despite this, I tried to quell the rising anxiety, reminding myself of Switzerland's legendary efficiency;

surely, they would sort everything out quickly. Nevertheless, to secure peace of mind and to address my existing travel arrangements, a trip to the station became a priority.

The twenty-minute walk was arduous due to heavy rain, though thankfully not snow. En route, I stopped at the information desk. While waiting, I glanced at the local news, despite being in German, conveyed a chilling truth: *The village of St. Nicholas, just below Zermatt, had been wiped out due to floods, killing around 100 people! The station staff, clearly overwhelmed, reiterated the dire situation: no one could enter or exit Zermatt until the tracks were fixed, which was delayed due to the relentless weather.*

Transport and communication had come to a grinding halt.

—

Embracing Destiny

The anxious hours sheltering in the church finally concluded as the downpour subsided. Pushing open the heavy door, I emerged into a world transformed by a blanket of knee-deep snow. I had resolved to secure an inexpensive lodging near the station to ensure the earliest possible departure from Zermatt.

After inquiring at several places, I checked into a small Motel by late evening. From riches to rags, but secure nonetheless. It was a minimalist room – a single bed, a rack, and a washbasin in a space the size of a small balcony. A shared bath and toilet lay down the corridor, and a basic breakfast was included. Its most vital feature: a window, overlooking the station, *my only hope.*

I jolted awake to the rumble of thunder and the flash of lightning. The storm outside was wild and unyielding. The streetlamp illuminated the relentless streaks of rain, each drop a tiny projectile against the glass.

My room was eerily silent, amplifying the frantic rhythm of my own pulse. Profound fear, cold and sharp, began to prickle my skin.

Was this really happening?

This wasn't a narrative I could control; it was a terrifying reality unfolding.

I tried to pour my thoughts into my journal, but a torrent of tears betrayed my forced composure. All day, I had waged a quiet war within, battling back the surge of this terrifying fear, refusing to invite it closer. Yet now, in the solitude of that small, dark room, the unknown pressed in, a suffocating grip of uncertainty tightened its hold. I desperately needed to find resilience, to hold onto the smallest glimmer of hope.

The shared washroom was at the end of the passage. The corridor's feeble tap light offered a mere ten seconds of illumination. A frantic sprint was required to reach the bathroom before being swallowed by darkness. Anxieties about the other guests and the vulnerability of being attacked filled my mind.

I clutched the room key, a small anchor of security. Even inside, the sensor light in the bathroom proved unreliable, plunging into darkness midway through. A scream clawed at the throat. I flew back to my room, heart hammering. I tried to find solace in a desperate prayer, conjuring images of home, family, and friends, longing fiercely to be back there. Eventually, exhaustion took over, and I fell into a fitful sleep.

The rains showed no signs of relenting the next day, indicating another night of uncertainty. Thankfully, a chance encounter with an American family – grandparents, parents, and their three delightful children – provided a welcome respite. Their invitation to share meals offered not only sustenance but also a comforting sense of safety and belonging, alleviating the dread of being alone.

Announcements, amplified by speakers and megaphones, declared that the train track repair would take at least a week to begin!

What! A whole week?

Panic flared through me – my flight out of Zurich to India was in just two days!

Quickly, I sought out the tourism board office and secured a vital letter detailing the delay. Looking back, that foresight was a lifeline; funds were running perilously low, and it was necessary to conserve enough for a week's unexpected stay. Mealtimes are now only a matter of necessity, involving skipping or meagre portions of just soup and a bread loaf.

That night, the rain was less intense but still a constant reminder of the situation.

—

Tides of Fate?

Awakened suddenly at 4 a.m. by an announcement on a megaphone from patrolling officers about airlift evacuation operations at sunrise and the need to collect a token. I went back with an alarm and went at 7 a.m. That was a colossal mistake!

Upon arrival, I was stuck in the serpentine queues that

stretched endlessly. The sheer number of travellers was astonishing, as I didn't see as many here since I had arrived. All were waiting patiently in line. While in the queue, I made inquiries to them, which yielded no answers as everyone seemed to be equally clueless. The atmosphere was tense.

After an arduous three-hour wait, I got my token bearing number 747. It was then that I got to know that only two helicopters were transporting passengers across the mountain, and, crucially, that payment was mandatory for the service.

Returning with my bags at 4 p.m., the scene was still bustling with a significant crowd. An announcement clarified that rain would cease all helicopter operations, which, even without rain, were limited to sunset due to the lack of night vision on these flights.

True to the warning, at 5 p.m., a heavy downpour began, sending everyone scrambling for cover or prompting their departure. The rain lasted an hour, and with sunset imminent, the majority left, advised to return the next day.

I wasn't ready to give up.

Not yet.

Once the crowd thinned, I nervously approached the office to inquire if the existing token was still valid or if I would need to re-queue. When she confirmed that fresh tokens would be issued, my hopes crashed further, and I desperately searched for any remaining hope.

Just at that moment, the distinctive sound of a helicopter approaching filled the air. The radio snapped with an announcement: "One last flight departing."

I needed to be on this almost-departing flight.

Instinctively, I produced the earlier procured letter from the tourism board and explained the urgency to reach Zurich for my outbound flight. She examined the letter, spoke on a walkie-talkie to an official, and her reassuring smile signalled an unexpected breakthrough.

"You can go; it seems they can accommodate you", she said.

Without a moment's hesitation, I emptied all my remaining emergency funds to buy my ticket.

—

Winds of change

Though this was my first ever helicopter experience, the urgency of the situation left no room for any thrill or novelty. The sun was just dipping below the horizon; the uncertainty of take-off was palpable. With silent hope, keeping my fingers crossed as the final passenger(me) boarded, with ten before me.

The short 15-minute flight ended unexpectedly in a remote, open field far from any habitation.

After getting off in the dark, the initial exhaustion gave way to relief as I realized that I was finally SAFE. A newfound energy from within, despite being utterly disoriented. I followed the anonymous crowd, wordlessly, carrying our bags, until we arrived at a bus stop. Caught the first bus to the railway station and secured a seat on the train that took me to Zurich.

Despite my arrival past midnight at the hotel, the message box overflowed with frantic notes from the entire family. I called my parents the moment I was in my room, and the sound of my mother's voice from across continents instantly gave profound relief and a powerful sense of security. My dad was reassuring and tried to sound more cheerful and less anxious. The subsequent conversation with them was filled with tears, born not of sadness but of immense joy and relief.

—

Epilogue

This unforgettable dramatic narrative with race against nature's forces and rescue against insurmountable odds is forever etched in my soul.

Adventures like these might seem like a singular lifetime occurrence. But earlier than this, there was an equally gripping experience when I faced an ordeal with a forty all-girls group: stranded at the border due to escalating political tensions... and what happened next?

That's a tale for next time...

~

12

I am Single, I am Happy, and I am Cocky!

~ Kaushal Patel

A true friend is ready to lay down his life for you unless you have already killed him.

Swirling the whisky glass in my hands, I looked at Subramanian Swaminathan Iyer, my childhood friend. He has come straight from the office, shocked and excited in equal measure about what has happened to him today. At first, I laughed at him, then I ignored him, and now I am getting pissed at him.

"Subbu, have you gone cuckoo?" I asked in perplexity.

"No, I haven't!" barked Subbu in retaliation. His voice was slightly slurry, which wasn't surprising given the speed with which he was downing his drinks.

"Zoruuu, you litt'l prick, trust me," he said animatedly, "the fellow was divine. He wasn't human; He was God."

Subbu is the most gullible and idiotic person I know. He has more trust and affection in him than logic and smartness.

We have been together since kindergarten, an age when bonds are formed intuitively, before social conditioning takes over . As such, we are opposites. He is an emotional fool; I am not. He sees the good in people, I am a narcissist; in our relationship too both of us love me.

Credit is due where it is – Subbu is non-judgmental and

accepting. He rarely complains to me about me. He ignores people, even Seema, who tell him that I am too much of an arrogant, sarcastic pig to be a good friend.

Well, people don't know, I am fairly easy to get along with once you accept my superiority.

"Ok, let's go over it again," I said and continued, "the boy, sorry, the God in denims, with headphones around his neck, helped you up when you slipped inside the metro, made you sit, and...?"

"*Yesss, riiiight!* Then he started talking," Subbu recalled, "Sometime during that soothing discourse, the background blurred and I could only see his illuminated face. The words rhythmically coming out of his mouth..."

"What words?"

"He said, *"I am granting you a chance. You can go back in time and stop an event from happening, either in your life or in someone else's. You can change history! Think and let me know."*

"Meaning?"

"Meaning, he would allow me to go back in time, to wherever I desired, and change whatever I wanted to change there. Like I could time travel to January of 1948, rush to Mahatma Gandhi and tell him, 'Watch out, Sir, Godse's got a gun!'"

I was appalled at the ludicrousness of the man. This was supposedly a 35-year-old, well-educated, even happily married – at least in his own eyes – talking.

"And so, I have to come to you, my *masterrr* Zoruuu, for thou wisdom. Help me decide what to do," Subbu implored.

Drinking makes Subbu touchier. Instead of debunking his bubble outright, I asked a logical question.

"So, moron, if all this did happen, how will you let your so-called God know your decision? You don't know where he is now."

Subbu looked up to me, "Mr. Zorawarr Mistry...you wise ass," his voice louder, slur stronger. "See this!"

He held his phone in front of me. A whatsapp chat was open from an unknown number. There was a single line of text which said, "Think about what you want to change. Send me a text here."

"What?" I asked incredulously, "Send a message? Like booking time travel online? God has his own travel portal now?"

"Zoruu, my brother, I know you think'm stupid," Subbu got up and came towards me, swaying slightly, "But God *musbe* identifying good-hearted people to bless..."

"Only cardiologists can identify good-hearted people, Subbu."

"Haha, I *luuuve your wit Zoru.*" He slumped down next to me. "Ok, now pay attention, brother, very important," he dabbed his fingers on my arms, "What should I change?"

All this was funny and irritating at the same time. Obviously, Subbu had met a fraudster who'd left this message on his phone, and once Subbu interacts on this number, something worse will happen to him, which will be the second time in recent years. The first time was when he got married to Seema. I couldn't stop that, but I must stop this, I thought.

"So, do you want to stop a big historical event or a personal event?" I played along while pouring both of us one more round of Scotch.

Subbu assumed an expression of deep intellect, a superhero making a grand decision for mankind.

"*Shouuuld* I, mmm, stop the India-Pakistan partition?" he asked

"How?"

"I can lock Mountbatten in the bathroom."

No point debating. "Let it be. We have just beaten Pakistan in the World Cup; the fun will go away."

"Tru... tru...," he agreed while pulling his phone out. It was ringing. He went out to talk.

The time is nearing 11.30 at night. It must be Seema checking on Subbu. I look at the Scotch bottle and assess that Subbu's probably downed six. Sentimental Subbu will blurt out that he's here, and Seema will blow her top.

I see Subbu stumble over the side table on the way back.

"Zoooruuu, don't worry, I am not drunk. Seema had called..." he started laughing, "...and boom," he gestured a bomb going off with his hands. "How badly I wiiish you both got along. Why can't you be *litt'l niice* to her?'

Poor Subbu. Seema and Zorarwar – two of the closest people in his life – don't like each other. But his one-sided accusation didn't escape me. Turning a blind eye to the spouse's behaviour must be one of the seven marriage vows.

"You rem'ber, when I first met Seema?" Subbu settled back on the couch.

"I do. June 2009. College farewell. You were roaming behind her like a puppy."

"Ya, I had liked her instantly. So kind-hearted."

"If I recollect, it wasn't only the heart that you'd liked."

"Haha, I *rem'ber* you quipping 'Wish you all the breast', when I went to talk to her," Subbu recalled

We both laughed out loud; men will be men.

On the topic, I have always found Subbu and Seema's relationship stressful to witness. The only time both of them don't argue is when they are sleeping or having sex. Both of them became my role models of an undesirable marriage. Hence, I am single, I am happy, and I am cocky.

"Subbu, I think you should get going," I remarked.

"No, Zooorru SIR! You neeeed to tell me what to say to that God?"

"Subbu, please understand. It's a trap. Stay away from it."

"Hehe... You'd said the same thing about my marriage. But see how happy I am now."

"Are you?"

"Of course, I am! Zoorru, you see, your stubborn idea of freedom and bachelorhood will not last you long. Trust me, you will soon need a companion," he said.

We exchanged a stare.

"Sorry, sorry, I forgot, you don't like to face reality. I am going to shhhhh...," he said, keeping a finger on his lips, which were wide open in a condescending smile.

Subbu was dangerously poking the giant Zorawar ego. It's one thing to judge me, that's fine, possibly I am that good. But to be ignorant about your own life, which has become a caricature after marriage, is living in denial.

"Zooruuu, what if I ask God to take me back to 10th grade

in school? I can stop Delnaz from shifting to Delhi. You can marry her, and all four of us can be family friends and live happily ever after," Subbu said, half joking, half serious.

Ouch, that hurt. That always hurts.

Subbu thinks that I have become whatever I am today because Delnaz and I could not continue our relationship together. Read differently, it meant that I had become self-centred, rude, and unbearable because Delnaz wasn't there in my life.

If only I could tell Subbu how his own life sucks after Seema. That... he is always under a cloud of stress. That... he laughs less and less now. That... Zorawar and Subbu are drifting apart, from best friends to mere acquaintances.

"Bro, I'll take a leak *n* come," Subbu got up with a struggle. "If Seema calls, don't pick up." He said as he left his phone on charge.

Subbu's phone did ring when he was away. But it wasn't Seema. It was a message from that Unknown number. I opened it. Just one word.

"Waiting..."

I stare at the message for a long time.

You see, history only records events; crucial decisions taken that eventually led to something. But it can't ever record the feelings and emotions the decision makers are in when they take those decisions. That's what will happen today.

The matter here is, Zorawar Mistry is way bit pissed with Subbu, and emotionally charged to prove how his own life is great, and how Subbu's life is not.

I decided that responding to this message is a great way to do that. Yes, it's most likely a fraud. Too bad for Subbu if it is. But just in case, it isn't, then Subbu will be saved, Zorawar will be proven right, and everyone will live happily ever after

I type – "June 2009, our college farewell. Wipe out my meeting with Seema." I check the response once more and then hit send.

I return to the couch and take a long hard sip of the scotch as I wait for Subbu.

—

My mind registers that it's morning but my body refuses; I have had restless sleep. I want to sleep more. I hear some noise, but I zone out. I move my legs. I feel something – another body. I sit up in shock and worryingly look next to me – What the..., a small boy is sleeping next to me. And, he looks like me! What's happening?

I hear a woman's voice at a distance "Zoru baby, come out for breakfast, Subbu's here." I hurriedly got up to go out.

My living room looks different. All my art is gone, replaced by baby pictures. Still reeling under the enormity, my eyes fall on Subbu. He's at the breakfast table, looking razor sharp and happy.

"Good morning, Zoru," he says

"What the fuck happened, Subbu?" I rushed to him. "Who's that?" I pointed towards the kitchen where a rotund woman was working.

"You don't know?" he smirked, "That's Mrs. Zorawar Mistry. And that," he said, pointing at a picture on the wall, "is Master Zorawar Mistry."

I want to collect my thoughts, but I can't find my mind.

"Don't be a smug Subbu. Tell me all. I will butcher you right here,"

"Dude, listen, I can only say thanks, my friend."

I take deep breaths. Calm down, Zorawar. "For?"

"For sending that message out last night. I went back to June 2009. I didn't meet Seema. It was a different experience of the same event. Amazing. You know, we went pubbing?"

"Okkk, so you are back in 2025, and now..?"

"I don't have Seema in my life. I am single, I am happy, and I am cocky!"

I was flabbergasted and shocked, and everything else that words can't describe.

"Great for you, Subbu, but how the hell did I come to all this?"

"It's simple when you look at it now, Zoru. When you change one event, it causes a ripple," Subbu discoursed, "This ripple in time moves the fabric of destiny. Events that follow after that are not in our control. It impacts everyone. Because I had undid my meeting with Seema, destiny took us to a pub that day. That's where you met Padma."

"What the hell?!"

"She's your wife now."

I look around with trepidation.

"Subbu, am I happy?"

"Shhh...," Subbu kept his finger on his lips, which were wide open in a condescending smile.

~

13

NDA - An Affair to Remember

~ Kajal Mehra

Now I am petrified of the reptile family. A harmless wall lizard, whom some endearingly call Lizzy, is someone to whom I have not gotten used and frankly don't want to!

Nestled far from the maddening crowds lies this utopian haven, which still continues to inspire and draw in newcomers from across the country. For the others who have a chance to call this their alma mater, it's only with a sense of heightened pride and sweet nostalgia, memories and playful times spent in the vast greens whilst getting inspired by the many quotes bannered on the high and mighty ceiling that gives the stature to this place. I am referring to the institute called NDA, the National Defence Academy, where one enters as a cadet and walks out as a tall officer beaming with nothing but a sense of pride, embarking on a long and arduous journey. And walk out they do, only to return time and again to their home away from home on occasions that bring back all those fond memories and stories to share and narrate, recall and pass on!

It pays to have family in the defence and grow up listening to their many stories, which speak of sacrifices, bold encounters, and challenges, amongst others. Not only do they sensitise you on the human front but also try to make you feel strong should you need to face the enemy – in my case, the creepies! A story about rescuing oneself from the coiled snake has not gone down well with me. Anyway, recently I had the joy and privilege to attend an occasion in this institution and listen to their many stories first-hand. This particular one happened to be the 60th anniversary celebrations of the pass-out batch of 1965! Now, normally these celebrations are only for the defence personnel and their immediate families, but I can say I was only lucky this year as they decided to invite the extended family, should they wish to, and I would say, who wouldn't juggle their time schedules to pack in this one? I am a big succour of these best-laid plans and jump at such opportunities. After all, living is all about gathering experiences and listening to heart-warming stories.

The first time I saw the camaraderie amongst coursemates was at this pit stop we all gathered at before entering the academy. My husband (he, of course, was an invitee along with me) and I were introduced to the many veterans. Saying hi and hello to us, they very quickly got down to talking amongst themselves as chatty little children would. The exchanges of pet names, endearing words for one another, and general banter amongst themselves felt like time had stood still in their existence. The passage of time adds so many memories, but some moments and days are frozen in time lines, and it's good that way. It takes one back to all and more, and the inner thoughts come to the fore, much sometimes to the chagrin and amusement of the others.

In one morning chai session with the senior citizens, I heard a playful tone of sorts in a conversation. An elderly Sardarji had given a tall order to his equally elderly fellow-mate.

"Arre, chal pagdi theek se bandhwa jaise pehle bandhwata

tha," said this gentleman.

"Kuch alag rahi hai ye pagdi," said the other. "It's not the complete length." Now the length of the cloth that is eventually tied up as a neatly fitted turban on a Sardar speaks a lot of his outward appearance. This turban was apparently not doing justice to the final look. The non-Sardar friend could see this very clearly.

"What to do now?" said the Sikh uncle. "Time has added wisdom to my head, but it has come at the cost of my long mane. I need a smaller length of cloth for my turban now."

Both had a hearty laugh at this, and I sat smirking and absorbing this small anecdote.

In the two days that we were engaged there with totally filled-up, timely calendars, one realised what it takes to be a person defending the country, braving the enemy and keeping us all safe. An interesting story was shared by the commanding officer about the evolution of women's role in the armed forces. He spoke of how initial reluctance had transformed into complete acceptance and admiration. Women, he explained, bring emotional courage and intelligence to the forces. It's not about which sex is stronger, he emphasised, but about those who encompass integrity with compassion and a heightened sense of discipline. It has taken a good almost 70-odd years to get women on board! Current times and tides have made this happen.

On one of the beautiful mornings that we spent walking about in the pristine greens that adorn this place, I spotted a rather secluded hut down a long driveway. Little did we know that we would soon return to this quiet and calm place for a solemn morning. This particular ceremony is held outdoors for a reason. A flame is lit by the defence personnel in memory of the dear departed in total state honours. At one point, it looked like the skies were ready to burst open, and there was a sudden scramble around to get some shelter. Now the gods sure have a way with the timing and sanctity of occasions, so for the 30-odd minutes that everyone wanted to pay their respects, he totally obliged with just the mildest of drizzles! We all could go into the hut and see and remember all those who had laid down their lives ever since our nation became independent. The dependency on them to safeguard the rest of us was seen with tears of pride and outstretched hands with flowers to shower on them. A serious and sombre air filled the surroundings, and for all the right reasons. Many of us intermingled and could hear soft mumblings and gentle murmurs. The walls were plastered with the heroic tales of the departed, and many short stories were there for us to read and absorb. Boy! What a morning it was!

Talking about mornings, let me highlight a very ear-piercing and shrill sound that used to wake us up. At the stroke of six, bagpipers would march up and down the corridors to make sure we were sprung up from the cosy comforts of the barracks! It was both annoying and fun at the same time. Took you on a Scottish town morning at no extra cost!

Yet another morning was earmarked to understand and see how the naval forces conduct their drills. The calm waters of the Khadakwasla lake was the chosen area. The drive to this point was impeccably dotted with many manicured greens. The ride was gorgeous, and upon reaching the earmarked location, we all disembarked from our vehicles. Inching closer to the water body, I could see signage of various sorts. The one that made my antenna really go up was "BEWARE! THERE

ARE CROCODILES IN THE LAKE." Now we were to be taken on that lake for a boat ride. Of course, it was known that only if it were safe would we all be taken, but somehow I felt, at this point, a meek lamb to the slaughter kind of feeling. What if the odds were stacked against me? What if something crazy happened? My mind, somehow, to avoid this, was beaten to death by the lively and brave people I was surrounded with. All along, I walked around with my head held high; here I felt a slump. This one place was literally giving me the jitters, being terrified of the reptile family! Nonetheless, I braved through the whole experience! There were a couple of dinghies lined up to take us all. The ride was both interesting and frightening at the same time.

As we were nearing our port of entry upon finishing this rather mind-scary ride, I heard a loud splash! And there the mind went into a tizzy. I knew the crocky was behind this! I closed my eyes to avoid seeing a pool of red. I do admit to watching too many films where such a scenario crops up! And with a silent prayer, looked around to see what the brouhaha was all about! Much to my amusement, it was a routine drill being conducted in the nearby dinghy, all to show us the safety and efficacy of all of this. Did my face reveal a sigh of relief, or did my welled-up eyes speak something? I don't know, but for sure this has left a memory so deep, it'll be hard to erase – and why should I erase it? Fear and vulnerability do run in all of us; just to see the bravehearts never show it makes you all in awe of this wonderful fraternity, whom we should look up to with admiration at all times!

What a fitting finale to this wonderful meet and greet: two full days with tall disciplinary orders followed impeccably, delectably curated cuisines, and wonderful evenings with music and melody. An experience to cherish a lifetime: the walls which have stood the test of time, the open grounds which have seen many a salute, the memorabilia which is entrenched here so deep, and the pride which leaves all of us smiling all through!

But amongst the company of so many bravehearts, I still have my angst moments with the creepy crawlies - the Lizzies!

~

14

The Wooden Curse

~ Mamta Agarwal

I was only four years old when the decision to send me to a boarding school was made. No, I was not an unruly child who needed discipline. Nor were my parents away from home most of the time. The reason was partly due to a lack of good schools in the city we then lived in, and mostly because my older siblings were being sent. It was more about convenience and seemed the logical way forward. Not that I complained. To be honest, I was as clueless as any four-year-old kid. Joining this early had its advantages. Settling in was smooth and linear as instructions were followed to the letter T. I soon became the pet of all the teachers. Being the youngest helped, but my knack for naming each teacher after a typical food item made me especially amusing and entertaining. All my teachers wanted to know their nicknames and the reason behind them.

Most of the kids befriended me, with some swearing that I was their best friend. They would confide in me without feeling judged. Being a good listener cleverly masked my inability to judge them at that precarious age. While my peers thought their secrets were safe with me, I never really remembered any within minutes of it being said. However, it worked to my advantage as my friends got a patient ear to vent.

I did have my share of downsides, too. Food and I could never be friends. Suppertime would be an ordeal. Mrs. Bowman, the mess-in-charge, would dread my mealtimes more than I. I soon learnt to navigate this. Food would be stuffed in my pockets only to be handed over to the older children. Till I was caught, and frisking became a daily routine. I resorted to the next innovative option. The food portion would be stuck under the dining table, hoping and praying that it would not fall off before I left. The lid on this got blown off in a few weeks, though. And this is when Pedro came into my life.

Pedro was the friendly and not-so-friendly (if he so desired) pet dog. He had been a part of the school way before I joined. Legends have it that his mother died after delivering him on the school's premises. He has since been adopted by the school as one of them. To set the record straight, I have nothing against dogs. Just that, I am not exactly fond of them. I am fine provided we both are within our segregated boundaries, doing our thing. The problem was that Pedro was now assigned to keep an eye on me while I was having food. My ingenious ways to dispose of the edibles then seemed almost impossible. Pedro's alert eyes would never blink, not for a second. There was just no way the food could be squeezed anywhere except through my oesophagus. And this meant taking hours to finish my meals. Somehow, the day would pass, but dinnertime would be the real deal.

As per school folklore, the place was haunted, and spirits got activated after 9 P.M. (An older me once set out to investigate if there ever was a non-spooky residential educational institution. I have miserably failed so far). My alma mater's setup consisted of two floors. The topmost was where the students resided. The first floor contained all the offices, including the principal's cabin. The ground floor was where the dining hall stood. There were two sets of stairs at the extreme ends to access the floor levels. One was stone and the other wooden.

For some strange logic, the stone stairs were inaccessible after 9:00 P.M., rendering the timber one as the only available option at that hour. The institution also had two playgrounds. The smaller front one was where most of our activities took place. The bigger one was used occasionally, mainly for sporting competitions. This field was rectangular for the most part, with a small aberration at the end. It was as if it were injured and was suffering from a sore. Though sore it was, as no one ever played on that patch. If, for any reason, a ball or a frisbee got accidentally thrown there, retrieving it would be a task. Somehow, that space evoked immense fear. It was believed that Pedro's mother was buried there. Of course, no one thought it necessary to verify this. It was universally accepted and passed on to any willing ear. It also happened to be Pedro's favourite place, adding to the story's authenticity. Nine out of ten times, if Pedro needed to be searched for, he would be found there.

The story circulating in the halls was that the ghost of an earlier principal would visit her office after 9:00 P.M. Apparently, something sinister occurred during her tenure, and the proof of her innocence lay there. She was credited with adopting Pedro's mother, Bosky. Both doted on each other. Every night, without fail, she would take the wooden stairs to search for that proof and soon get violent when she failed. In a fit of rage, she would attack whoever was present, either in the hall or on the stairs. Bosky, her devoted puppy, would follow suit. Many students had reported hearing footsteps and sighting a screaming lady charging towards them. A few even claimed to have been attacked. Bosky's presence there added to the chaos. Pedro would wail loudly from his favourite spot during that time as his mom was missing. We certainly heard Pedro wailing night after night consistently. The entire scenario seemed surreal. The bottom line was that no kid ventured this way post nine, unless necessary. That too either in pairs or a group. Going solo was simply out of the question.

So, when my dinner hours got stretched, it posed a challenge daily. The fear did not instill a sense of promptness in finishing my meals, as it should have; rather, it made me use all the leverage gained earlier into coaxing someone or the other to accompany me up those dreaded stairs. The method was simple. We would all sing loudly in unison and make a dash for the stairs at full speed. We held hands and made sure we all travelled together. The sounds were there for sure, but couldn't overpower our frightful singing. We believed that if we stopped, the spirits would attack us. We were convinced of hearing a shrill shriek occasionally. All this combined with Pedro's incessant wailing. The moment we reached our destination, it gave a sense of accomplishment – yet another sequel of "Mission Impossible."

Soon, my luck ran out. Every single person refused the routine of this exercise. I was left with no choice. No, I still did not finish my dinner quickly, but decided to brave it out. Sooner or later, I anyways had to find a solution. I was quite optimistic that once I crossed this hurdle alone, it would be a breeze henceforth.

Gathering all my might, I walked towards those stairs with eyes half closed, believing that the less I saw, the easier it would be. The thumping of the wooden steps could be heard loud and clear as I reached the base. It was as though someone was making a cacophonous leap, eager to get hold of me on finding me alone. In that instant, I ran up with all my might, making a feeble attempt at crooning a popular track, which sounded so ghastly, it was as if the ghosts were singing for me.. The thumping too matched my decibel levels, getting louder and louder by the second. Was it my heartbeat? The situation didn't warrant any reasoning, as my brain urged me to run as fast as my legs could carry. Suddenly, an arm tapped on my shoulder from behind. Refusing to look back, I continued charging forward, half stumbling and dragging myself on. The tap felt harder and stronger. I could feel its grip holding me back. Only a few more steps, I told myself, yet I could not move an inch. I tried the next best option -to scream louder, but right at that very moment, my vocal cords decided to ditch me. A pair of hands suddenly gripped me tightly and all I remember after that was a loud thud and darkness thereafter.

When I regained my senses, the nurse and the matron were fussing over me. I was running with a high temperature. Apparently, I had passed out on the stairs. The memories of the previous night, though, were crystal clear. I did hear, see, and feel something. Pedro, too, had done his bit.

The only silver lining after this episode was that a lot more empathy came my way. Dinners were more relaxed, and my servings were reduced. I was allowed to leave with the others, even if it meant carrying leftovers. I never had to go through the 'wooden curse' way – as it was called – ever. As the years flew by, stories about the ghostly experiences continued to float, some far-fetched but giving similar vibes.

I soon graduated to other chapters of my life with two little munchkins of my own. Many moons later, I got an invitation to a school reunion, which I immediately accepted. My excitement was palpable. I wanted my children to meet my childhood friends' children and relive it all over again.

I was surprised to find the wooden staircase missing on reunion day. It had given way to a more state-of-the-art elevator. I was barely admiring the modernization of my alma mater when Keerti interrupted my thoughts. She was one of my early school friends who had decided to serve the school that gave her so much. Our chat gently veered onto the 'wooden curse' topic.

She gave her usual throaty laugh, amused, "How we believed that one! Ah, the age of innocence!".

I just stared back, perplexed. Had I not experienced every bit of it, the memory of which still gives me goosebumps? Was she suggesting that I had imagined it all? I protested.

"Nah, you didn't make it up. The stairs were completely dismantled once they had weathered beyond repair. Guess what was lying underneath? A rat hole, literally. There were so many, all in varying sizes. Rats are known to get active at night. That explains the thumping sounds. Besides, wood tends to either expand or contract based on the weather conditions. That explains the creaking and screeching sounds", Keerti elaborated patiently.

"Wait!" I continued with my dissent. "What about the tap on my shoulder? Who do you think held on to me that night?".

"The only logical explanation is that you froze and imagined this bit. Given your age and circumstances, I'd dare say it isn't unusual. I would also have been overwhelmed. Believe me, ever since the stairs have gone, the noises and occurrences too have ceased. Not a single incident has been reported since.

"And what about Pedro?" I continued, rattled.

"He is no longer with us", she quipped.

However difficult I found it to believe, she did make sense. Besides, the madness had stopped. I was only too happy to get some closure on a childhood trauma. We laughed off the frivolous flapper of childhood. The clock had already struck nine, and my kids were famished. We bade our goodbyes with promises to catch up soon.

As I was exiting the school premises, I heard it again. There was absolutely no mistake here. The wailing of Pedro could be heard loud and clear.

~

15

Women in Uniform

~ Chandni Bhatnagar

It was International Women's Day, and I was to receive an award from the Government of New Delhi for saving over a thousand lives at sea during my service in the Indian Coast Guard. As I buttoned up my pristine white ceremonial uniform, a smile played on my lips. Years of storms, operations, and relentless service had led to this moment.

The uniform clung to me like a second skin - starched, pearly, and sacred. I glanced in the mirror, adjusting my peak-cap with practiced precision. Medals gleamed like tiny constellations against the crisp white fabric, each whispering its own tale of courage. My name-tally sat with exactness, simple yet carrying the weight of duty. My white ceremonial shoes, spotless and glowing, had been gently cleaned, marks erased with care, as if handling crystal footwear. The uniform felt enchanted, whispering silent stories.

In the military, a uniform is more than attire – it is armour, identity, and pride. It reflects discipline, sacrifice, and honour. Before one speaks, the uniform speaks of missions faced, lives saved, and the unwavering spirit of service to the nation.

Behind my polished exterior were years of hard work, sleepless nights, life-saving decisions, high-risk rescue missions, and daring medical evacuations. Sometimes, cries of families desperate for news of their loved ones lost at sea echoed in my mind. I remembered the gratitude in the eyes of poor fishermen when I brought their loved ones back alive. "Thank you, Didi, for saving our family," they would whisper with folded hands and tearful eyes. Those moments, those lives – they were my true medals.

That day, all the toil had taken tangible form. The award was more than a trophy; it was a symbol of every storm weathered, every mission successfully executed, and every life saved. I felt proud, not for myself alone, but for every young girl who dared to dream beyond boundaries, for every officer in the line of duty.

As I stepped out of my apartment, folder in hand, I was greeted by the familiar morning-walk circuit – a group of aunties gathered near the park, gossiping and enjoying the early breeze.

"Beta, you're a true role model for every young boy and girl – such grace, such aura!" exclaimed Rajni Aunty, her face glowing with pride.

Before I could respond, the ever-watchful Anu Aunty stepped forward, eyes narrowing with concern. "May no evil eye fall upon you!" she murmured, circling her hand in front of me, following the age-old ritual meant to shield against envy and misfortune that often trails admiration and success.

But the evil eye apparently heard her. Loud and clear.

My car was parked nearby, and as I walked towards it, the folder clutched tightly, I felt the warmth of many eyes following me, not just admiration, but genuine affection. These were the people who had seen my journey unfold, from a playful child to an officer in uniform.

As I entered my car, feeling the quiet weight of the uniform and the significance of the day, I put on my favourite song and softly thanked God for the moment. My heart brimmed with gratitude for leaders and colleagues who had trained me, for the sea that had tested me, for the lives I had saved, and for the chance to serve. I only hoped to make a difference – and that day, I felt deeply blessed.

I drove to the venue, heart steady, uniform crisp, the invitation beside me like a passport to a moment I had never imagined. Upon reaching the gate, a security guard stepped forward and asked to check my ID. He scanned it, looked puzzled, and said, "You're not on the list." I calmly replied, "I have the official invitation." The confusion deepened until I realised the issue – he had mistaken my rank, Commandant, for my name, and couldn't find "Chandni" on the list. It wasn't his fault – this sometimes happens when a woman wears a rank not commonly seen.

Once inside, I parked the car, gathered my folder, and stepped out – only to be met by an unexpected "aerial strike." A pigeon, perfectly timed and tragically accurate, released a direct hit on my shoulder. The white of my uniform made the mess glaringly obvious. I froze, horrified. Today, of all days, when I was the face of the event, my uniform was marked by bird droppings.

Panic swelled, but I quickly found a restroom, cleaned the soiled part with water, and used the hand blower to dry my uniform. The stain had faded but not disappeared. Still, I stayed calm – I had faced far worse. Compared to midnight emergencies and real danger, this was just a minor obstacle.

I walked in – steady, composed, and even a little amused.

At the reception desk, I was greeted with warm smiles and a crisp "Welcome, Ma'am," and promptly escorted to the Awardee Box – a front-row seat among distinguished guests. Around me sat trailblazers, champions of their fields, all polished, poised, and celebrated.

Only to face yet another challenge.

As one awardee's name was announced, he leapt up in excitement and, while squeezing past me in the narrow row – BAM! – his shoe landed squarely on mine.

CRACK!

My white ceremonial shoe's heel broke. Just like that. Was it really crystal?

I stared down in disbelief, eyes wide, mouth open, on the verge of tears – but the uniform doesn't allow crying, only problem-solving. My foot throbbed, my pride took a hit, but my instinct took over.

My service had been full of Search and Rescue missions. Now, I launched a personal Search and Repair mission.

I had left my peak-cap on my chair in the Awardee Box, intending to return in just a moment. Hobbling away like a wounded warrior, half-laughing, half-crying, I found salvation in the green room: a bottle of glue and a stapler. Simple office stationery – now my emergency toolkit. Gluing, stapling, and praying with military focus, I repaired the heel. It held. Stable, not perfect, but enough. Chin up, pain buried, I returned – mostly on my toes.

But my seat was now taken. And my peak-cap? Missing.

"Was there a cap here?" I asked the new occupant.

"No, there was nothing here when I took the seat," he shrugged.

Swallowing my rising panic, I approached the event coordinator. "Did you happen to see a cap on that seat?"

"Yes, Ma'am! I saw it unattended and placed it on the cap stand."

I rushed to the cap stand, eyes darting, and found a white cap with a golden emblem. I lifted it, only to realise it wasn't mine. No name inside. Someone had taken mine and left theirs.

Just then, my name was called.

I sighed and shoved the oversized cap on my head. It sat too low, nearly covering my eyes. Yet, I squared my shoulders and marched to the stage.

The announcer's voice echoed:

"Today, we honour Commandant Chandni Bhatnagar of the Indian Coast Guard, the first female officer and Deputy In-Charge at the Maritime Rescue Coordination Centre, Mumbai..."

"...She has led various rescue missions, saving over a thousand lives from the unforgiving sea. As a Woman in Uniform, her contribution to maritime safety has been nothing short of extraordinary – saving lives, and proving that courage knows no gender."

The final call came: "May I request the Chief Guest to present the award to Commandant Chandni Bhatnagar?"

As I stood, the weight of the day hit me. A pigeon strike, a broken heel, a glued shoe, a lost peak-cap – and yet, I was still standing tall.

I walked towards the stage, cameras flashing, the glued shoe holding, the oversized cap wobbling. But my face was calm. This, too, was military life – smiling through chaos, solving problems with grace, and carrying on with composure.

On stage, I shook hands with the Chief Guest, received the award, and smiled. I wasn't thinking about the mishaps anymore. I thought of the sea, the lives saved, the missions endured. The uniform had endured stains, cracks, and swaps – but never my resolve.

That night, as I folded my cherished uniform, I smiled through tears. The uniform had shaped me through trials and triumphs – and in return, it had made me unbreakable.

To every woman dreaming of the uniform, I would say: wear it with pride, with fire, with purpose. Because to be a Woman in Uniform is to rise through chaos, to lead with courage, and to become the storm when the world expects stillness.

~

16

Our Unfinished Stories

~ Nirali Hathi

That morning began like any other, as Isha joined her family at the breakfast table, a steaming mug of tea warming her hands. As she sat down, relishing a bite of tangy-sweet baked beans on crispy, golden toast, she had no idea that she was about to embark on an unexpected journey through time with her fifteen-year-old daughter.

As they chatted about their recent days, the conversation drifted to the tiffin menu for the upcoming week. Her daughter's eyes, typically glued to a screen, lit up with excitement as she listed her favourite dishes one after the other. "Mutter paneer," she declared first, already picturing the cubes of cottage cheese mixed with her not-so-favourite green peas in tomato sauce. Next on her list were "quesadillas," and her eyes twinkled at the thought of melted cheese oozing between crispy tortillas. "And aglio e olio," she quipped. "My friends love it too," she added, envisioning the fragrant garlic and olive oil clinging perfectly to al dente pasta.

At that moment, something stirred within Isha. She couldn't help but reminisce about her childhood. The flavours of pav bhaji and the comfort of aloo paratha – dishes that graced their tiffin boxes only as a rare treat once a month – came flooding back. Back then, they weren't just meals; they were edible experiences, often wrapped in old newspapers and packed inside otherwise predictable steel dabbas. Those memories felt like treasures – so different from her daughter's modern-day food choices, yet both showed how food continues to bridge generations.

She found herself transported back to her school days. She envisioned herself sitting in the middle of a bustling classroom, surrounded by lively classmates, debating an insignificant topic. A vivid image formed before her blurry eyes: neat notes jotted down in a single-line notebook, with a black-and-gold Hero pen – one of the most prized possessions of her time – resting beside it on a slightly wobbly wooden desk.

The image grew clearer and sharper, and within no time, the blackboard at the front of the classroom appeared before her, covered in formulae scribbled in coloured chalk, half-erased from the morning's maths lesson. "That was all we had," she thought, smiling just as the doorbell rang, snapping her back to the present.

A courier had arrived, delivering a pen drive sent by her daughter's friend for a school presentation the next morning. As Isha handed it over, another wave of memory hit her.

They, too, had tools for sharing and storing data – bulky floppy discs and shiny CDs – proudly burnt with files, songs, or videos downloaded through agonisingly slow dial-up internet connections. Back then, every successful CD burn felt like winning a gold medal. Once complete, they would label them with colourful pens – sometimes glittery, sometimes scented – adding their stamp to something proudly crafted. Back then, the world was slower, yet it had its charm.

Stationery was not just functional – it was personal.

Flaunting more than three sharpened Natraj pencils, scented erasers, the latest box of colour-changing sketch pens, or a shiny new geometry box, each item was quite a status symbol. And if it bore a 'Made-in-foreign' tag, one was treated like royalty. Even if half the items were never used, the pride of ownership was enough.

One memory stood out vividly – a pack of crayons, gleaming in shades of gold, silver, and copper, sent by her aunt. They weren't just colours; they were treasures from another world. After all, they were imported and had come all the way from London. Each crayon felt like a rare gemstone, and Isha handled them with the utmost care, shielding them from the curious hands of friends. Once, when a dear friend innocently reached out to use one, her heart sank. She was so upset, she nearly stopped talking to her!

Those little things – the geometry box, the fancy erasers, the imported crayons, the Hero pen – weren't mere objects. They were small symbols of pride, love, and care. They were proof that childhood wasn't just about growing up; it was also about learning to cherish something deeply, even if it was just a shiny stick of coloured wax or a fragrant eraser.

That same sentiment lingered even today, even if the items had evolved. Her children still doted on their precious stationery. Just the other day, Isha had watched her ten-year-old son scrolling through an app on the tablet, searching for options to order blow pens and brush pens, carefully reading reviews to find the best deal for the best product.

Meanwhile, her daughter was gently using her newly purchased set of pastel dual-tipped highlighters to mark important sections in her textbook. After use, she meticulously put them back in their packaging, as though tucking them into bed. Every night, Isha watched her jotting down thoughts in a lilac sequin notebook, using the glitter pens that adorned her bedside. Before beginning, she would gently dust them, treating them with the same care Isha had once reserved for her treasured belongings.

Watching her, Isha smiled and realised one thing hadn't changed with time: the joy and protectiveness felt towards possessions. The objects may have changed, but the attachment hadn't. Whether it was a pack of metallic crayons from London that Isha treasured as a child or a set of pastel highlighters and brush pens ordered from an online store, the excitement of new stationery remained timeless. Prized possessions – whether new or old – were always cherished and given extra care.

Wasn't life truly a full circle? As she observed her daughter arranging her stationery, tidying her desk, and recording tiny memories in her notebook – often during lectures she and her friends found boring – Isha felt as though her daughter was reliving fragments of her past while gently crafting her own story.

She was trying to hold on to time, to make it last a little longer. Isha could see her building a collection – a collection of glances exchanged across noisy classrooms, of scribbled notes passed beneath desks, of laughter echoing in old corridors, of secrets sealed with BFF promises, of dreams dreamt between the bell ringing and lunch breaks, of heartbeats frozen in pictures, Insta stories, and Polaroids, of goodbyes wrapped in tight hugs and teary smiles – a collection of fragments that would one day be called 'the good old days.'

But those 'good old days' wouldn't just be about the treasures held – they'd be about the hands that held theirs, the voices that called their names, and the friendships that quietly shaped who they became.

As her daughter stepped into her final school year, Isha could already sense what the future held. The world her daughter knows today might scatter tomorrow. Some friends would chase dreams, ambitions, careers, and responsibilities. Some would move cities, some would shift countries, and some might drift away with the changing currents of life.

Isha's life had changed after school, too – just as her daughter's was about to. Printed photographs were forgotten and tucked away in drawers, along with slam books scribbled with messages from Grade 10. From the daily hustle and bustle of the classroom, her classmates and she had transitioned into the quiet calm of adulthood, leaving behind the versions of themselves that existed in their teens.

But life had a curious way of circling back. What it took away, it sometimes returned in unexpected ways.

It surprised her, too.

For years, those connections had remained tucked away in her subconscious, resurfacing through rare chance encounters – a friend request, a tagged photo, a message in a group chat. With a new wave of technological change sweeping in, smartphones and social media platforms emerged, becoming the bridges they never imagined they'd need.

Old names popped up again, along with familiar faces frozen in profile pictures. Slowly, forgotten jokes, classroom mischief, secrets, and gossip returned – this time through group chats. The versions of themselves they had outgrown began unfolding once again through shared memories. Friendships scattered across time and geography began to rekindle and find their way back.

As Isha reflected on her journey of drifting apart, of losing touch, and then reuniting through smartphones and social media, she could only smile with gratitude. Just as she and her friends had found their way back to one another, she knew her daughter and her friends would too. They'd reconnect, reminisce, and laugh over the same stories told a hundred times. Only the medium might be different. Who knew – years from now, her daughter might slip on a sleek pair of AR glasses, step into the metaverse, and find herself attending a virtual reunion dinner, laughing with her school friends, perhaps even holidaying with them as digital avatars.

The tools may change, but the longing remains the same. We all carry our people, our places, and our pasts with us, in whatever form technology allows.

After all, life has a gentle way of circling back.

~

17

Checkmating Chaos: Krishiv's Game of Time

~ Krina Gala

Krishiv, a 10-year-old chess prodigy, was best described as hardworking, disciplined, and full of dreams, yet secretly exhausted from trying to keep up with the world's relentless race.

School, thankfully, was a different story. He actually liked going there. He loved math (Shhh... don't tell anyone). Solving problems was a breeze. But life outside the classroom? That was chaos.

Everyone around him, young or old, seemed to be surfing some invisible wave. Gaming trends changed weekly. New slang popped up faster than he could Google it. It was like the world had forgotten to slow down.

On one rainy evening, Krishiv sat by his apartment window, watching raindrops fall into the sea. The waves rolled in and out with a comforting rhythm.

"At least the tide is reliable," he murmured. "Up, down, in, out. Always the same. Why can't life be like that?"

No amount of thinking could solve the mystery. So he turned, as he always did, to his beloved escape – chess. The one place where time paused until he made a move.

Behind him lay his heirloom chessboard, passed down through generations. He could still hear his grandfather's voice from the day he gifted it to him:

"Every game you play on this board, Krishiv, will teach you something about life."

As Krishiv set up the pieces, the day's frustration flooded back: an argument with Mom over screen time, a fallout with his best friend Aarav, and, worst of all, not getting picked for the school athletics team. He sighed. "Time's going too fast. People are changing. I'm stuck."

Suddenly, a knock.

But not from the door.

It was coming from the chessboard.

The white knight stirred. The bishop yawned dramatically. The rook stretched his stiff corners. The queen adjusted her crown while the pawns grumbled awake.

"Finally," said the black king. "You're ready." Krishiv blinked. "Wh-what's happening?"

"You asked a real question," said the white queen, her voice elegant and knowing.

"And this board was made to answer it," added the knight.

"Time is a tide," the knight continued, "but chess teaches you how to ride it – how to pause, pivot, protect, and push."

A quiet gong echoed. White made the first move.

Move 1: Pawn to e4

Krishiv moved the pawn.

It squeaked, "Every tide begins small. The tiniest step can

create the biggest wave." He thought of Aarav, who hadn't spoken to him since he accidentally revealed Aarav's crush in class. A genuine mistake... yet it had led to three long days of silence. "Maybe I should talk to him first," Krishiv muttered.

The pawn nodded. "Make the move."

Move 2: Knight to c3

The knight galloped forward.

"Time doesn't move in a straight line, neither should you!" it called. "So instead of saying sorry," Krishiv said, "I should challenge Aarav to a chess rematch? No words. Just moves?" "Exactly," the knight grinned. "Knight logic."

Move 3: Bishop to c4

Krishiv sliced the bishop across the board. He thought of his mom, of how he always ignored her when she asked for help, always had a screen in hand. Maybe instead of arguing, he could surprise her. No speech. Just action. "Bishop energy," he whispered. "Small moves matter. Act early. Outrun the tides of regret."

Move 4: Castle

The rook and king switched places.

"Let the storm pass without letting it in," the rook said. "Castling isn't cowardice. It's wisdom."

"You mean... take breaks?"

"Exactly. Say no to what drains you. Focus on what builds you. Rest smartly."

Krishiv grinned. "I'm officially reducing my screen time starting tomorrow."

"Respect," said the rook, saluting him.

Move 5: Queen to h5

The queen glided across the board with elegance.

"In life, time gives you two choices," she said. "Wait and worry, or act and grow."

Krishiv's eyes lit up. "So... if I want to try out for the athletics team, even though people think I only play chess, I should go for it?"

"Indeed," the queen smiled. "Let them be surprised."

Final Move

The king stepped forward."Don't fear the ticking clock," he said. "Use time. Plan your moves well."

"But what if I fail?" Krishiv asked.

"Then fail boldly," the king replied.

"Failures are just waves hitting rock. They polish you over time. They prove you're still standing."

"Like my science test. I scored 6 out of 15," I added.

"Exactly! That means you have 9 more points of learning to collect," said the king.

Krishiv chuckled. "Nice spin, Your Majesty."

He made the final move and won the game. But the king simply smiled. "That was the least important part."

Krishiv frowned. "Then what was?"

"You," said the king. "You changed."

The board shimmered. The pieces bowed. Then silence.

Just before freezing, the queen whispered, "Life isn't about fast wins. It's about timing your moves with the tide."

That night, Krishiv tossed and turned, trying to absorb all that had happened. By morning, life was back to normal. He didn't tell anyone... who would believe a talking chessboard?

But as he stood on the balcony that evening, gazing at the sea, he whispered: "I don't need to chase time. I just need to play my moves right."

And that's exactly what he did.

He called Aarav for a playdate and challenged him to a game of chess.

He helped his mom set the breakfast table without being asked.

He even traded 30 minutes of screen time for reading. His mom nearly fainted.

And yes, he submitted his name for the school's annual athletic meet tryouts.

Krishiv realised every mistake is just a wave polishing him into something stronger.

As the tides rise, time flows steadily. But if you learn to play your pieces wisely – pause, protect, pivot, and push forward – you'll always stay in the game.

And life?

It's all about staying in the game, even when the world doesn't expect you to.

~

18

The Changing Tides

~ Kruti Sharma

There's a photograph Kruti keeps tucked into an old leather-bound notebook. In it, she is seated at a workstation in a high-rise office, headset tilted, blazer crisp, smile practised. That was her – twenty-six years old, working for a large firm, caught in the comforting rhythms of corporate life. Deadlines, meetings, team outings, appraisals. A well-oiled machine. She thought she had it all figured out.

Back then, ambition was a sharply dressed woman who never missed a beat. Kruti admired her from afar, trying to imitate her poise and confidence. But something about her days felt borrowed, as if she were reading a script written by someone else. Her work was respectable, her pay cheque steady. But a whisper inside her, soft and persistent, began to grow louder: "Is this it? Or can I build something of my own?"

She ignored the whisper for a while. After all, who walks away from stability to chase a dream that has not yet taken shape?

And then she became a mother.

Motherhood, she had been warned, changes everything. What she had not expected was how it would transform her sense of identity. She was not just navigating sleepless nights and nappy bags; she was meeting a new version of herself. One that craved freedom, not just from a 9-to-5, but from limits she had not realised she had placed on herself. Time, once a relentless to-do list, slowed in moments with her child. There was room now for reflection, for wondering, for dreaming again.

That is when the whisper became a calling.

She began exploring the idea of starting a business. Training had always fascinated her – the alchemy of words, energy, and intention transforming a room full of people. She had conducted internal sessions at work, and each time, she felt more alive than she ever did while working on spreadsheets or attending project calls. She remembered how participants leaned in when she spoke, how eyes lit up with recognition, how a shift happened – not always visible, but deeply felt. She wanted more of that.

And so, between baby naps and late-night research, Kruti sketched the beginnings of what would become her training business.

It started small. One workshop here, one session there. She became certified in POSH (Prevention of Sexual Harassment), then in soft skills, image management, and communication coaching. Her calendar, once filled with client meetings and internal reviews, was now peppered with sessions on workplace dignity, confidence-building, and leadership communication. The transition was anything but easy. There were days when she missed the security of a fixed salary, when she questioned her decision, when she wondered if she was being foolish.

But the tide had turned. And she had begun to sail.

What shaped her more than anything else was not the certifications or the courses – it was the people. From housewives taking their first steps into the workforce to CEOs navigating complex boardroom dynamics, she stood in front of them all, a mirror and a messenger. And each one, in their vulnerability and courage, taught her something about respect.

Respect, she learned, is not hierarchical.

It does not come dressed in a title or wear a tie. It shows up when a shy homemaker gathers the courage to speak English for the first time. When a senior manager admits, "I do not know how to lead with empathy." When a group of field workers sit through a POSH session and realise for the first time that dignity is not optional – it is their right.

There was a moment during one such training that stayed with her. She was conducting a POSH awareness session for a group of factory workers. One woman, in her mid-40s, raised her hand hesitantly and said, "Madam, nobody has ever asked us how we feel at work." Her voice cracked. The room went still. That day, Kruti did not just train – she witnessed healing. And she carried that moment with her into every workshop that followed.

Time has passed, tides have turned, and her business has grown. She now works with corporates across India, designing programmes that go beyond checklists. She walks into boardrooms and classrooms with equal intention. She helps build safer workplaces, and she does it not just as a trainer, but as someone who has seen the power of transformation up close.

She often thinks back to the young woman in the photograph. That young woman had dreams she had not named yet, and fears she pretended not to feel. Kruti wants to tell her it is okay to be uncertain. That life is not a straight road, but a river – sometimes rushing, other times meandering, always moving.

She wants to tell her that time is not the enemy. It is the tide that carries us where we are meant to go, if only we are brave enough to loosen our grip on the shore.

Today, Kruti stands not just as a business owner, but also as a witness to the many shades of human experience. She has spoken with interns and CHROs, with field staff and executives, and in every conversation, she has found stories shaped by time. People who dared to change, who chose to listen, who rose from failure, who led with kindness.

In her own journey, she has made mistakes, learned hard lessons, and rebuilt her voice. She has balanced client calls while heating baby bottles. She has cried from exhaustion and smiled through self-doubt. But she has also felt the quiet triumph of independence, the joy of making a difference, the respect of being truly seen.

If there is one thing the tide has taught her, it is this: we are all in motion.

Our stories are not defined by a single role, job, or phase. They evolve – as we do – with time, with courage, with the willingness to begin again.

So here she is. A mother. A businesswoman. A POSH trainer. A corporate coach. A woman who once doubted her dreams but followed them anyway.

And tomorrow? She will become someone else again.

Because the tides do not stop.

And neither will she.

~

19

To Risk or Not to Risk!

~ Dr. Usha Jayachandran

An unusual incident in Udhampur has left a remarkable imprint on my life.

Born into a defence forces family, I am the elder of two children. Dad was a disciplined army man, and his postings every two to three years took us to various corners of the country. Just when we were settling down in a new place, we would be uprooted from our schools and circle of friends, giving us, in return, the invaluable experience of learning how to make new friends and adjust to unfamiliar environs.

It was never easy, as the postings were mostly to small and remote places in India. But as kids, we took on the challenges thrown at us with a sense of adventure and nonchalance!

During one such posting of Dad's, we found ourselves in the beautiful climes of Udhampur – a scenic valley nestled amidst the snow-clad mountains on the way to Srinagar. The army cantonment was located in a lovely spot, with bubbling streams flowing through the mountains. We were allotted the ground-floor apartment of a one-storey building.

It was a unique experience. We had never lived in a valley before, and the natural beauty of the place had us mesmerised.

My brother and I used to walk to school every day. It was

about a kilometre and a half away from home, and Dad was very clear – the army jeep allotted to him was not meant for us to be indulged with rides in!

On our way to school, we had the option of either walking along the main road or taking a shortcut across a wide stream. The walk across the stream – hopping atop rocks that formed a haphazard path through it – was one of the highlights of our morning routine.

Although the school had warned us that when glaciers beyond the mountains melted, or during heavy rainfall, flash floods were a real danger, the adventurers in us always chose the thrilling route over the safe one beside the highway.

It was on one such adventurous morning that my little brother and I learnt a life lesson.

It had rained all night. The morning was drizzly and cold, with a cloudy haze that had wrapped itself around the mountain tops. We woke up a tad late. It was one of those mornings when you just wanted to snuggle under the blankets and stay put.

Realising we were running late, we scooted out of the house – our backpacks jostling on our backs – and sprinted towards the main road, a few yards away.

The highway was eerily empty. We realised that the school buses we usually saw enroute had likely reached our school by then. The usual group of kids we walked with was missing too. They were probably already in school.

When we reached the fork in the road – one path leading to the shortcut across the stream, the other along the main road – I tugged at my brother's arm, nudging him gently toward the shorter route. Sensing our delay, and fearing the wrath of the prefects and the punishments that would follow our late arrival, he followed me without hesitation.

The inclement weather and the risks involved were playing at the back of my mind, but I believed we could make it!

When we reached the banks of the stream, I noticed a definite swell in the water levels. Still, the flow seemed calm and steady. Looking across to the other side, the distance didn't seem too long. Jumping atop the rocks and crossing the stream safely seemed pretty doable.

Some of the rocks closer to the far bank, usually well above water level, seemed to be submerged in an inch of water. That daunted me slightly. My inner core was still in a dilemma, but the musketeer in me got the better of my judgment.

Upstream and downstream, there was no one in sight, except for the white and brown spotted mongrel we often saw lounging on the rocks. It usually skipped and jumped happily when it saw us, giving us cheerful company.

Today, it sat on the opposite side, amidst a mound of tall grass, watching us intently.

I glanced upstream. The water didn't appear to be flowing any faster than usual. So, I took the plunge – stepped onto the first rock and began our crossing.

As I pranced onto the second rock, I felt water ooze through my shoes and wet my socks. I shrugged it off and continued, focusing on the task ahead.

A quick glance back told me that my brother had also stepped onto the first rock. He was staring hard at the next one, his sceptical expression catching my attention. I paused

– were we doing the right thing?

Still, I jumped onto the next rock, and then the next, with my brother following close behind – like a little lamb mimicking every leap its mother took.

With every step forward, more water seeped into our shoes, and splashes danced around us as we tried to balance on the uneven rocks. That day, the rocks seemed more submerged than usual. A creeping sense of foreboding began to set in.

My gut told me to turn back. But we were already halfway across. The water had risen to our ankles, and our toes were soaked in the icy current. Our minds coaxed us to hurry, our eyes fixed on the rocks between us and the far shore.

Then, glancing to the right – upstream, from where the water flowed – I saw, to my horror, a huge wave rolling down from the mountains. It snowballed into monstrous swirls.

I froze, paralysed. I stood stuck to the rock I had just landed on, unable to move.

My brother, unaware of the danger surging towards us, leapt onto the same rock and grabbed my hand.

"Didi, come on! Let's move fast and cross the stream! We're getting late for school – we'd better hurry!"

Before we knew it, we were swept off our feet by the torrent, flailing helplessly as we were tossed about by the current.

I could hear the mongrel barking frantically, running along the banks in the direction the water was pushing us. Its barks were frenzied, desperate – as if calling for help.

What happened next is inexplicable.

We found ourselves caught in a huge net that seemed to have appeared out of nowhere. We clung to it for dear life. I held onto my brother's shirt collar while he hugged me tightly in a bear-like grasp. Our heads bobbed just above the water, and then I felt strong arms grab me.

A voice yelled above the roaring water, urging me to let go of the net and trust that we'd be saved.

After what seemed like ages, we were finally pulled to safety. As I sat on the banks, being gently towelled down, I realised we were surrounded by a few personnel from the armed forces. They had rescued my brother and me from a near-death catastrophe.

We later found out that the mongrel's barks and its frantic run along the banks of the stream had alerted the army men. They had foreseen the bad weather and the potential for a flood and had placed safety nets downstream as a precaution.

When the mongrel raised the alarm, they sprang into action.

We were asked for our parents' names and address, and were escorted home in the army jeep, no less. Not quite the exciting reason one would hope for a jeep ride!

On seeing my father, the rescuers immediately saluted him and handed us over, leaving us to do the explaining.

That was a fortuitous day for the two of us, the Udhampur adventurers.

While our disciplinarian dad was understandably upset, he sat us down and calmly explained the importance of not taking dangerous risks. Rather than risking our lives, he said, it was far better to be late for school and face the consequences.

That year, my brother and I became notorious across the cantonment as the two little bandicoots who had dared to challenge the twists of Mother Nature – and were rescued by the army!

We were mini-heroes in our school for having faced the wrath of the stream and lived to tell the tale.

Don't take risks when the dangers are obvious, and never think it can't happen to you. Life is too precious – value it, never risk it!

That life lesson from Udhampur stays with me even today. I never mess with my gut feeling anymore.

As for the saviour mongrel, it became our friend forever. From that day on, it trotted along the main highway with us, walking to and from school, the moment it saw us approach the fork in the road.

~

20

Trekking upwards & inwards...

~ *Vandana Narang Lund*

Bhutan, the land of happiness and health, was beckoning! Simplicity, warmth in smiles, nature, abundant beauty, temples, and monasteries – all promising true comfort and solitude to a tired soul. For years, we had been planning this trip, and it was finally happening.

"Are you ready for this?" my husband asked over breakfast at our hotel, his eyes twinkling with excitement. Dad, seated opposite me, smiled.

"As ready as I'll ever be," I replied, though we all knew that trekking up to Tiger's Nest Monastery was not for the faint-hearted. For someone like me, who wasn't a regular trekker and preferred walking at a comfortable pace, this would truly test my patience, determination, endurance, and willpower.

After a light and healthy breakfast, I decided I would climb as high as I could. My rucksack was light, and dressed in simple attire, I was ready to embark on this journey, not knowing what lay ahead. I love it when life unfolds and surprises you in such ways.

Walking through the greenery and dense forest vegetation, the three of us reached the foothills of the mountain together. I was amazed by the variety of trees and plants surrounding us, and the chirping of birds was music to my ears. That morning felt particularly special – there was a sense of freshness and clarity in the air.

"Right then, shall we begin?" Dad said with characteristic enthusiasm, adjusting his walking stick.

We started the trek together, continuing to march ahead with faith that we would make it to the top. Walking slowly yet steadily, I knew I would soon be left behind. My father and husband would inevitably be way ahead, yet I didn't want to give up, at least not at the very beginning.

They were wonderfully kind and supportive, slowing down their pace for me to catch up. We stopped frequently, soaking in breathtaking views, appreciating the nature around us, and occasionally chatting with fellow trekkers we encountered along the way.

"Look at that view!" I called out, pausing to capture a photograph. "Isn't it magnificent?"

I love to live every moment as if it's my last. I found myself slowed down by unique varieties of insects and birds perched on branches of stunted trees. I enjoyed capturing moments and taking photographs, finding myself smiling for no reason. My mind had slowed down completely.

By this time, I hadn't realised that I was all by myself; Dad and my husband had walked ahead. Just for a moment, I panicked, not knowing where or when I would see them again. I was deeply immersed in my thoughts when a complete stranger noticed I looked rather worried.

"Don't worry," he said gently, his weathered face kind. "There's only one path to trek up and down this mountain. You'll meet them soon enough."

Setting my worries aside, with courage and a prayer in my heart, I carried on walking and enjoying myself. As I reached higher altitude, I found myself gasping for breath, sipping more water, yet keeping my spirits high. May was surprisingly cold in Bhutan, yet I was perspiring. I felt charged up and determined to make it to the top.

After about two hours of trekking, I decided to take a little break under a shady tree to gather my thoughts. It's in such natural surroundings that one truly experiences solitude. The realisation dawned on me: man, in his pursuit of progress and growth, has ventured far from his roots, and from HIMSELF.

Immersed in my thoughts, I continued my journey uphill. There, I was pleased to encounter a group of mountaineers wearing matching t-shirts, carrying their gear and rucksacks, happily singing and walking along effortlessly.

"Mind if I join you for a bit?" I asked.

"Of course! The more the merrier," one called back cheerfully.

I walked with them for a while before continuing on my solitary journey. I was truly enjoying my own company and listening to my inner voice, which otherwise sounds quite muted in the daily grind. The various shapes and sizes of boulders and rocks were fascinating, with messages engraved on some – travellers love to leave their mark and imprints in time.

Further uphill, I encountered a group of trekkers who appeared very sad yet calm. My heart sank as I learnt they had lost one of their companions to cardiac arrest. Their medical kit couldn't provide more than basic first aid.

"We're heading back to base camp," one of them said quietly. "Please, be careful up there."

"I'm so terribly sorry for your loss," I replied softly. "I'll keep you all in my prayers."

They decided to walk down whilst I walked ahead with a prayer in my heart for the departed soul. My mood had shifted. I was no longer focusing on the greenery and vibrant hues of nature; instead, I noticed dry leaves, patches of barren terrain, and I even stumbled upon a dead jungle cat. Life seemed to be reflecting what I was feeling.

With tremendous perseverance despite physical fatigue, I reached where people were sitting and relaxing in a giant circular structure – the only café at the top. Here, one had access to basic food, water, and soft beverages to regain strength and the will to march on. Due to sheer exhaustion from climbing the steep incline, some people were even having a little snooze.

I sat down, grabbed a snack, and started planning ahead. Reaching this café felt like a real achievement. I was surrounded by mountains on all sides, deep valleys with shrubs and flowering plants, and I spotted a mountain goat in the distance. Most remarkably, I watched a mother with her baby tied to her back, walking towards the summit as if she had walked this path a thousand times before.

In this amazing setting, I felt compelled to journal my thoughts like never before. By the time I'd finished putting my reflections into words, my husband appeared at the café on his return from Tiger's Nest Monastery, which was right at the summit.

"How was it?" I asked eagerly.

"Absolutely incredible," he said, slightly out of breath. "But getting there was rather tricky – you have to be extremely alert and vigilant not to miss a step. The path going up is very narrow, with thorny shrubs and wild vegetation on both sides."

Due to his regular gym workouts and fitness level, he'd reached the summit in record time. Shortly afterwards, Dad caught up with him, having stumbled a couple of times along the way.

"Nothing serious," Dad assured us with a grin, though his back was clearly aching. "Just reminded me I'm not as young as I used to be!"

After they'd had their much-needed rest, we began our descent with confident smiles, determined to return before sunset. The trek down was much easier; however, the soil was now wet from rain, and we were careful not to slip. Keeping our backs straight whilst walking on the steep slope remained strenuous.

"We did it!" Dad exclaimed as we made our way down. "What a team!"

The three of us were clearly meant to be on this journey together, and we returned with a sense of accomplishment that was truly extraordinary.

Life is rather like this trek – sometimes an uphill struggle with unknown and some known companions along the way. It shocks and surprises you with various twists and turns. One moment you hear yourself clearly, and the next, you're drowned in external chaos. Nature and its unique creations help you stay grounded.

The journey to the top is usually undertaken alone, and it can become lonely at the summit, as it was at Tiger's Nest Monastery. Very few people venture that far; most, after stumbling a few times, like I experienced, turn back. Only the most agile and fittest muster the courage to complete it alone.

I also realised that letting go is tremendously important. If I hadn't done so that day, I would have slowed their progress, and they wouldn't have reached their goal. Yet another valuable insight emerged: you don't have to reach the very top to find happiness. I was utterly content with the journey and enjoyed every moment along the way.

Tiger's Nest Monastery, for me, became a journey within... time spent with myself that I thoroughly cherish and relive during times of distress. Every so often, I travel alone to recharge and reconnect with myself through memorable experiences.

The key is to learn from life, maintaining an open mind and a happy heart that yearns for nothing but the very best life has to offer.

~

21

Tidewalk

~ Anjana Chabria

As a psychologist, I've spent years helping others navigate their emotions, fears, and pain. I understood grief, loss, and resilience – so I thought I did. Then came the day everything shifted. A diagnosis. Cancer. Suddenly, time wasn't something I tracked between therapy sessions or calendar months. It became something else entirely – something I noticed in hospital corridors, in waiting rooms, in the mirror. I wasn't just a professional anymore. I was a patient. And in the months that followed, I began to understand life, strength, and myself in ways I never had before.

The first few hours after hearing the diagnosis are still a blur. It felt like life split into two parts – before and after. It was a whirlwind. People kept using words like 'strong' and 'brave', but inside, I was just trying to breathe through each hour. My mind, usually balanced and steady, felt cluttered with questions: How bad is it? What will treatment look like? Will I be okay?

Even as I sat across from doctors explaining procedures, scans, side effects – some part of me was watching it all from a distance, like it was happening to someone else. I gave myself a day to cry, yell, curse – to just vent. I didn't fall apart. But I did lie awake at night, staring at the ceiling, trying to make sense of what this meant for my life, my work, my kid, my family.

Being a psychologist didn't make me immune. If anything, it made it harder. I was aware – painfully so – of every emotion as it showed up. Denial, bargaining, fear, anger, helplessness. I knew the theory. Now I was living the reality. And that was something else entirely.

Treatment was to begin the next day. I had tickets to a comedy show. I almost didn't go. The thought of sitting in a crowd, laughing, felt out of sync with everything going on inside me. But I'm so glad I did. That night, the jokes, the laughter, the friends by my side, gave me something I didn't realize I needed: lightness. It didn't erase the fear, but it reminded me I was still me, and that joy could exist even on the edge of something unknown.

In the weeks that followed, my circle held me up. My brother became my quiet constant. He didn't say much, but he was always there at appointments, at chemo sessions. The daily calls and messages from my sister, bhabhi, and cousins all helped boost my morale. My daughter checked in twice a day, every day – morning and night. Her stories, her voice, and her steady presence from miles away helped me through the worst moments and gave me reason to smile when joy felt far away. My nieces, taking time out from work, making sure they come and see me, their very presence cheering me up. Feeling loved.

My friends rallied in the best way possible – not just with calls and messages, but with presence, laughter, and thoughtful gifts: soft T-shirts, skin creams, flowers. They made me laugh when I felt grey, distracted me with nonsense when I needed it, and sat with me when I had nothing to say.

At home, my parents, dealing with their own health issues, their own fears, were fiercely present. They anchored me in routine and care. They didn't fuss, but they noticed everything. A cup of tea at the right time. A quiet "How are you feeling today?" Their support was steady and deeply felt.

In many ways, the people around me reminded me of parts of myself I couldn't always access. They reflected strength when I felt weak, and normalcy when everything felt strange. And somehow, all of that became part of my healing, too.

Treatment came with its own rhythm – tests, infusions, blood counts, side effects, and more waiting than I could have imagined. Time no longer moved in weeks or months, but in cycles. The hours after chemo. The days until the next scan. The meals I could keep down – or even taste.

Some days, I felt strong. Focused. Grateful. Other days, I couldn't recognize myself in the mirror. The fatigue was unlike anything I had known – bone-deep. There were moments of nausea, pain, anger, and vulnerability I wouldn't have known how to name, even as a psychologist. And yet, I pushed through. Not because I was brave all the time, but because I had to – one day at a time. That has become my mantra.

There were small wins that felt enormous: a day without side effects, a walk on the terrace, an appetite returning. I learned to celebrate those small but significant victories. I also learned to listen to my body in a way I never had before. Rest was no longer indulgent – it was necessary. The hardest part was trying to maintain a positive mindset amid all this adversity – managing the fight within my own body, and within my mind.

And while I had the tools to understand the emotional toll

– the anxiety, the occasional dips into despair, the bouts of anger, the uncertainty of it all – I also realized that knowing and experiencing are not the same. I had to learn to let people in, to ask for help, to let myself be cared for. That was hard. But necessary.

Looking back, I'm surprised by the resilience I found in myself. Not the loud, defiant kind. But the quiet kind. The kind that keeps showing up. That keeps choosing to try. That keeps moving, even with fear beside it. I had never thought of myself as a brave or resilient person, even though I had fought seemingly endless battles in the past. This shift in perspective helps me to this day.

Cancer taught me that strength isn't a singular act of courage; it's a collective effort, a tapestry woven from love, patience, and vulnerability. I learned that I could be my own strength, yes, but reaching out and leaning on others amplified it. Letting my family, my daughter, my friends, support me didn't make me weaker – it made me whole.

It's been almost 2 years since diagnosis, and time feels different now. I no longer count days in appointments and chemo cycles, but I value the quiet, ordinary hours. I still look in the mirror and see the woman who stood bareheaded in the sun, unafraid of the world's gaze. That woman is me... scarred, but stronger than I ever imagined.

~

22

3 – 6 – 9 – 12

~ Parizad-Srivastava

He wasn't particularly good-looking, or popular, or even a great athlete. He was just another ordinary boy amongst the two hundred boys in her year, whom she had known since nursery school. She hadn't noted whether or not he was assigned to her classroom each year, at least not until that first assembly of eighth grade. She was standing, as usual, towards the end of the girls' line – at 5'7" she was always amongst the tallest in her class – when she looked over to the end of the boys' line to see a new face. Except it was a face she had seen many times before, on a much shorter, plumper body.

My goodness, he had grown lean and tall over the summer, and that longer hair really suited his face, and why hadn't she noticed earlier that his eyes had that hint of green, and why, oh why, was she staring right at him! She looked away, flushed, and tried to appear very interested in the warning the new foyer coordinator was giving them about being late for school, even though her eyes kept disobeying and checking out the boy six inches to her left. But then, she just had to turn and look up at him again when they began singing the 'Twameva Mata' hymn. Was that his deep voice? Her sudden movement must have caught his eye, because now he was looking down at her with a look of confusion, or perhaps amusement. She must have held her breath for the rest of that assembly because she felt quite faint by the time they had finished singing the last 'Jaya He' of the national anthem. The next day, she swapped places with the girl standing in front of her so that he was out of her direct line of sight.

Looking back, that was probably the moment she had 'fallen' for him. However, for the next three years, she didn't permit herself to acknowledge it. Even though she found herself being just that tiny bit more self-aware of how she was standing or what she was saying whenever he was in the same space, they never spoke to each other. Still, she noticed him. He was always so respectful, a loyal friend, and so very shy that she found her heart beating faster for him whenever he was asked to speak in front of the class. Outside the classroom, they had little in common. He was part of the National Cadet Corps – she loved seeing him in uniform – on the relay team for his schoolhouse (Einstein House), and always carrying around one of those T-squares and tubes for his technical drawing class. She, on the other hand, was on the debate team and the dance troupe and became captain of her own house (Tagore House) by the time they reached the tenth grade. Their paths rarely crossed.

And then came the dreaded board exams. Her seat assignment was in the huge Art room on the fourth floor. On one side, she had a bolted hexagonal window – God forbid anyone looked outside during the exam – and on the other side, seated six inches away from her, was *him*. This was the first time they were in such close proximity since that assembly three years ago.

"All the best," he said, those kind greenish-brown eyes, nervously smiling at her. As if nerves about the board exams weren't enough, her heart was now racing at twice the speed. She mumbled something she hoped sounded like "same to you" or at least "thanks," but it was probably just gibberish.

Right then, the invigilator banged the duster on her desk, announcing the beginning of the exam. Everyone flipped the paper in front of them and started to read the questions that would come between them and a decent university admission. For the next two weeks, they sat next to each other, filling their answer booklets with facts about science, Shakespeare, Europe, and maths. After each exam, they would pass their judgment on how it went: "That was tough", "Not too bad, right?" or "I'm glad that's over".

On the final day, he didn't show up. She was getting quite worried until she remembered that it was the sixth subject exam. He was probably in the technical drawing classroom while she stayed put for her economics paper. As the final paper was handed in to the invigilator, a huge cheer of joy erupted from all the students. She looked over to where he would sit and felt a pang. Was yesterday the last day she would ever see him? She looked for him in vain as she left the room and down the many staircases until she reached the canteen, where the teachers had arranged an ice cream treat. There he was, with two Vadilal vanilla ice cream cups.. They spoke for exactly three minutes about the exams, summer plans, and where they hoped to go to university before she realised she would miss her school bus.

"Let's stay in touch", she said.

"I'd like that," he replied.

She only realised that they had missed exchanging phone numbers when she reached home.

—

Six years later, an invitation appeared in her inbox. *"Let's meet at school to enjoy unlimited 'canteen vada pav', pineapple or coffee flavoured 'Energy' and reunite with batchmates you have lost touch with".*

He was the first person she thought of. Everyone was to arrive in their house colours. Mustard yellow wasn't the most flattering colour; however, she found a flowing white dress with tiny daffodils on it, which both fulfilled the dress code and showcased her long legs and slim figure.

She entered the Main Hall, as memories of all her plays, dances, and debates on that stage flooded her mind, and who should she find standing center stage? This was probably the first time he had ever set foot on that stage! She immediately pictured them playing the leads in a romantic comedy, hugging in the final scene, brushing against his lean torso under that Einstein-blue shirt. She shrugged it off.

"This is the first time I am seeing you in something other than grey and white", said an oh-so-familiar voice, holding the oh-so-familiar cups of vanilla ice cream.

They spent the rest of the evening catching up. He had indeed gotten into that university and was now a fully-fledged architect working at his father's firm. She had been in New York studying filmmaking for most of these years and would start as a second Assistant Director on a Bollywood film next

Monday. It felt so natural for her to lean closer to him when the crowd got too loud, singing some old Bryan Adams song, and just as natural for him to wipe off some ice cream that was apparently on her cheek. They slipped out to get a drink at 'On Toes' right as the group started bellowing: "To this our school we are proud to belong...".

She didn't admit this to him, but in addition to being her first crush, he was also her first real boyfriend. She had unconsciously compared all previous prospects to him, and no one had ever matched up. On their six-month anniversary, he became her first lover, and she felt like the happiest girl on the planet.

The next day, she was informed that the scheduled shoot in London had been moved up. She left Mumbai two days later. The time difference and the cost of international calls proved too heavy a hurdle, and once she heard her next assignment would keep her in London long-term, they decided to end things. They coined it a 'happy breakup' and tried to stay in touch over the next several years. Facebook helped, but he hardly ever posted. Then one day, she posted a photo with a ring on her finger in front of a California vineyard. She sent him a digital wedding card, though they both knew he wouldn't really attend her wedding in the Bahamas.

She kept an eye out for any life updates from him, but other than that building he put up along Marine Drive, she didn't hear much. Her heart skipped a beat when she saw his first-ever comment on her feed at the birth of her daughter: "She looks just like you".

—

Life in New York with a toddler and a constantly travelling husband wasn't easy. She had to leave her job, but five years later, it felt more like she had left her career. Then she got that call that every daughter living abroad dreads: "Papa had a heart attack. Come soon." It was only when the flight landed the next day that she realised that she hadn't been in Mumbai for nine years! She called her mum as soon as she landed and was relieved to hear that the operation had gone well; however, they weren't allowed to visit the ICU ward for another five hours. It was just as well, because her baggage never appeared on that carousel, so she had time to shop for some basics to tide her over.

She had just paid for her new set of underwear and toiletries when she heard a recognisable 'hello' from the man standing in the next payment aisle, his arm full of kurtas in various colours. She leapt up and hugged him. It was the tightest hug she had experienced, well, since the last time she had hugged him. As his hands wrapped around her waist, the kurtas dropped to the floor. She looked up into his brown eyes with that unique twinkle of green and felt tears flowing down her cheeks. Forehead wrinkled with concern, he ushered her out of the store and into his car parked right outside.

Over lunch, she told him about her life in New York with a cheating husband and how stuck she felt without a career to lean on to independently support her six-year-old daughter, still in New York with her in-laws. Then, suddenly realising the time, she asked him to please drive her to Nanavati Hospital to see her dad. Seeing her father's smiling face and the relief in her mother's eyes, she allowed them to convince her that she ought to go home and rest. She stepped out of the ICU ward only to see him still in the waiting area. They embraced for over five minutes; words were not needed.

On the way home, he drove by their alma mater and stopped at her favourite ice cream store with a knowing smile. They walked around the perimeter of the school, hand in hand, ice cream in the other hand, as she turned the conversation to how he was doing. He was to be married next month. He had pushed it out as much as possible, but being 32 and unmarried in his Gujarati community was just unacceptable. He had only met the girl a few weeks ago, and they had gone out to one dinner before their engagement ceremony at his home.

"Are you in love?" she asked in a teasing tone.

"How could I be?" was his very genuine response.

Eyes still locked on hers, he asked: "Are you in love?"

She responded with an affectionate kiss. The electric kisses that followed sent shivers down their spines.

They made a pact that these nine days would be their gift to themselves before attending to their big responsibilities. A gift they would cherish guilt-free and then never look back. On the last day, he kissed her on her forehead at the airport and said, "Promise me you'll do what's needed to be happy?" She nodded and made him make the same promise.

—

It was the final day of their mother-daughter adventure in Italy, celebrating her daughter's eighteenth birthday! Cinque Terre had truly lived up to being called the Italian Riviera. The multicoloured houses seemingly stacked on top of each other against the green waters were simply magical. As she gazed over the terrace at what promised to be another glorious sunset, she heard a familiar voice frantically shouting out her name. There he was, running after his little daughter, who took to hiding right behind her chair.

Both the 'Alishas' looked up at him at the same time!

"Hi Amit."

Over the next twelve minutes, they recapped their last twelve years, the births and deaths, marriage and divorce, and new career paths, but mostly their eyes just took each other in.

"Happy"? he asked softly.

"Very," she responded as her little namesake dragged him back towards his wife and son, appearing in the distance.

Her heart was glad to see that the past decade had been kind to him, too. As he walked away into the sunset, he looked back and blew her a kiss. She blushed as she returned it and waved goodbye.

Then she turned to her very amused daughter and related the story about the 3-year crush, the 6-month relationship, and the 9-day romance that led to this 12-minute happenstance.

~

23

6:00 P.M. of September 18th

~ Gayatri Hingorani

3:15 P.M. of September 18th is a lazy minute that basks in harsh sunlight and looks up at the world around aimlessly, with no interest in changing its course.

At the Good Luck Corner, it's the moment when Nargis Daruwalla, owner of *The Turning Wheel,* sighs deeply and looks outside the solitary window of her 10 feet by 20 feet pottery studio. She has not had a single customer since the girl from the College of Fine Arts came in five days ago. As a token of appreciation for all the information Nargis shared with her for her thesis on *Ceramic Sculptures: History and Appreciation,* the student bought a small vase. Nargis had crafted that vase herself more than a decade ago for the exhibition *Clay as Canvas.*

Those were the days when Shezaan, her husband and proprietor of *Sheer Sanitaryware* next door, would wallow in pride at the artistic creations of his wife. Every piece fresh out of the kiln had to be passed under his microscopic eyes before it was put up for sale. Some were instantly termed *Masterpieces by my Noorie* and prohibited from joining the shelf queue. But now, all those masterpieces have dried and hardened to unbreakability.

Shezaan had not stepped into the studio for months now. They always had lunch in his part of the shop, and that half hour was interrupted with business calls – mostly him shouting out terse orders to his team of five assistants. Selling bathroom fittings had never seemed a more onerous task. Nargis would soon retreat into her little corner, gifted to her by her loving husband on her 40th birthday. It was a wall he had gifted her – literally and figuratively, as time proved.

Time is like the judge on the pedestal, in its black robe and white wig, doling out words of wisdom in no shades of grey, leaving no room for any interruptions. So before you know it, the springy 4:00 P.M. of September 18th has arrived with a cool breeze under its arms, along with the scent of jasmine from a faraway tree. It carries with it the warm anticipation of things to come and settles at the brightest spot of Good Luck Corner – that of Sangeeta's *New Fashions,* adjacent to the *Sheer Sanitaryware* showroom.

Sangeeta, chief designer and owner of the shop, was bent over her desk, carefully examining the sequins that one of her tailors had stitched onto the soft mal fabric of her customer's saree blouse. In the air was the sweet smell emanating from the incense stick lit near the photograph of Goddess Lakshmi. Sangeeta especially loved working on saree blouses. It was the heart of the saree. So entangled would she get in the threads of the fabric that she often wouldn't notice when her own saree gently slipped off her shoulder, revealing a hint of cleavage – a spectacle that caught the attention of her coterie of tailors.

Sangeeta often corrected her customers when they referred to her as a "dress designer." She would profess that a true designer can't express her creativity in just one medium. By this spirit, she had designed and decorated her small shop herself.

The three walls were painted olive green, except for the highlight wall on the side, which was a deep shade of maroon. On it stood photographs of all her lovely creations, interspersed with posters of famous Bollywood celebrities in costumes that inspired Sangeeta. Alia Bhatt, Deepika Padukone, and Kareena Kapoor adorned her walls, but the centre spot was reserved for her favourite siren, Priyanka Chopra, dressed in a sleek mauve saree from one of her older movies, *Bluffmaster*.

Sangeeta had also set up a small divan with multi-coloured cushions in one corner for her customers to rest their haunches as they tirelessly waited. To complete the look, there was a hookah-style lamp on her desk that made the shop seem like an Arabic den right out of an item-girl song sequence.

4:20 P.M. of September 18th is a sinister little thing. Just a minute long, but full of deep, dark mysteries as it travels in the Tata Sumo of Umesh Upadhyay, the burly, shawl-clad local MLA. The big car was racing against time towards Good Luck Corner, where, in an abandoned garage adjacent to Nargis's studio, Umesh held confidential meetings with his henchmen. Today, the huddle was called all of a sudden. He had something important to convey and wanted them to gather at 6:00 P.M. sharp at their regular covert meeting place. No one was to know of the meeting except the inner circle. Umesh had torn himself away from a family picnic in Lonavala and was in a hurry to sort things out before they got out of hand.

The strained, cardboard-thin wall between *Sheer Sanitaryware* and *The Turning Wheel* was a disgruntled soul at the fleeting 5:05 P.M. The intense emotion between its two sides had caused cracks to appear on its surface. And Nargis and Shezaan had nothing to do with it. *Sheer Sanitaryware* was opposed to the move of being divided into two unequal parts. The Turning Wheel was now a separate entity, and the larger parent room from which it spun off was rather displeased at this separation. It missed the fullness of its being and would often, in those unsparing afternoon hours, push the hot air against the miserable wall.

The Turning Wheel, on the other side, was a bored little space that would have much rather been part of the complete entity. It would hear the buzz of people and clanking of objects on the other side of the wall and remember those days when it was part of the big story – and not just a small, uninteresting side plot within it. It would push at the wall too when the depression of its sole occupant, combined with its own frustration (of being as useless as the pots of different shapes and sizes that it contained), got to it.

5:38 P.M. is a slow minute that stretches in the time between the afternoon that ambles along quietly and the evening that holds much promise. It's also the minute when Jagral Pandey is just a minute away from Good Luck Corner, but it seems like an eternity will pass before he gets to it. Jagral, the postman, suffers from slowness – a disease that leaves its targets with painfully pronounced movements.

Jagral would do simple activities such as brushing his teeth, washing his teacup, and lifting the mail to be delivered, in the time that an average person would do it ten times over, if not more. With e-commerce flourishing and post-boxes going out of fashion, Jagral should ideally have made the lucrative move like his peers in the post office had eons ago. But, aware of his impediment, he continued to be loyal to his menial livelihood.

But Jagral was an optimistic man. Every morning, he set out hoping he would be able to complete his quota of mail delivery and still have time left over in the day – and that he would keep getting better at it until, one day, he became the flying super-postman that he often dreamt of.

And I'm 6:00 P.M. of September 18th, the protagonist of this story. I'm the time that people refer to as the "twist of fate" or "the turning point" because I make things happen.

Just before I come into existence, Umesh Upadhyay's secret meeting is interrupted by a group of gun-toting masked men who seem to have not paid attention during shooting class.

I'm the one who stands unguarded when the misfired bullet goes past the garage hideout through Nargis's cute little studio. I triumphantly see Jagral overcome his lifelong handicap as his sharp hearing and sharper sense of trouble guide him to quickly push Nargis – and the letter she is holding from her pottery teacher in Coonoor – away from the line of fire.

I also happily see that life-snatching piece of metal go past the thin wall between the sanitaryware showroom and the studio, causing it to crumble and create a hole large enough to open new channels of communication.

But unfortunately, that far-reaching bullet finds its innocent victim. As it races past the sanitaryware showroom into the outlandish den of the lovely designer Sangeeta, the bullet is smitten. It rushes towards her and lodges itself right on the alluring navel of the dusky actress.

The poster first jerks out of place, hangs crookedly for a split second, and then decisively tumbles onto the hookah lamp. Everything comes crashing down, as does poor Sangeeta, bent over her work desk as always.

I'm the moment that witnesses her saree fall off her shoulder, a fleeting glimpse of delicate white skin – before the smirk on my face gets wiped off forever.

~

24

KENJI

~ Zeyd Ladha

On a grey, drizzly morning, Kenji alighted from the bus. This was the starting point of the hike to Kinkaku-ji, a monastery high up in the mountains. He took a deep breath as he looked up at the monastery, which looked like a speck.

'Oh boy! That's a long way up!' he thought. He glanced at his watch and started his journey. There was a light mist blanketing lush trees. The birds sang a sweet song to the tune of a rumbling stream. A few hundred metres into the hike, he realised this wasn't going to be easy. The track was mucky, rocky, and uphill. At one point, his foot got stuck in the slimy mud.

'Why do they have to build the monastery up in the mountains?' he grumbled. 'They could just hold their sessions in town. As it is, life is difficult.' His mind went back to the last couple of weeks. It replayed all the challenges he had faced and then travelled ahead in time to what needed to be accomplished in the coming week. Kenji had surely split up. His body was hiking through a beautiful forest while his mind was stuck at his workplace.

—

Engrossed in thoughts, he reached the monastery. Before entering the premises, he turned around to see how far he had come. He was pleasantly surprised.

'That is a long way indeed!' he said, proud of his effort. 'Never thought I'd make it!'

He entered the monastery; it looked surreal.

"Excuse me," he said to a monk dressed in a maroon robe. "I am here for the meditation program and don't know where to go. Can you guide me?"

In a soft voice, the monk said, "Follow me."

They approached a big hall and stopped just outside.

"You may freshen up and return to this hall," instructed the monk. "And don't forget to leave your baggage outside."

"Where do I keep my bags?" asked Kenji.

"It wasn't about the bags," said the monk, and went inside.

—

Kenji returned to the hall and took his place. The participants waited patiently for the sensei. A few minutes later, Sensei Minato walked to the front of the gathering. "Good morning, everyone," he said. "My name is Minato, and I will be your guide through this journey."

Sensei Minato was a highly revered monk. Through years of meditation and practice of mindful living, he had reached a considerably advanced spiritual stage. Looking at the pressure and stress of modern life, Minato of Kinkaku-ji monastery had specifically designed this program. He intended to carve out a path that every person could take towards better mental and physical health. They charged no money for the program; instead, they demanded time. Participants who enrolled had to be there every weekend till they felt better. Even after that, there was no stopping anyone. All were welcome to go there as many times as they wanted and stay for as long as they wished.

—

"Welcome," continued Minato. "The fact that you are here means you are serious about your well-being. On the first day, I would like to hear from you. So, one by one, please tell me about yourselves."

One by one, the participants introduced themselves and spoke about their lives and concerns. Some mentioned their worries, while others talked about their health. Some cribbed about sour relationships, others about stress on the professional front. Kenji stood up when it was his turn and bowed to Sensei Minato.

"We have met earlier, haven't we, Kenji?" asked Minato.

Kenji was shocked. "How do you know who I am? It's miraculous!"

Minato chuckled. "I don't know who you are, I just know your name."

Kenji scratched his head in confusion.

"I saw the name tag on your bag," he smiled.

"Oh!" Kenji laughed. "May I ask you a question, sensei?"

"Sure, go ahead."

"You asked me to leave my baggage outside, but it wasn't about my bag. I did not understand," said Kenji.

"What I referred to was your mental and emotional baggage, the one that you carried all the way up here. You hiked up through the beautiful forest, but tell me, did you notice the songs of the birds? Or the rustling of leaves? Or the fragrance of the wet soil?"

"No, I did not," replied Kenji, feeling embarrassed.

"There's nothing to be embarrassed about," said Minato. "Let this be our first lesson. To live a happy life, you must learn to live in the moment. If you constantly carry regrets of the past and worries of the future, you will miss this beautiful present. So, when you are hiking through a forest, be fully in the forest."

Saying this, Minato stood up, and the participants followed.

"You may all retire to your rooms," said Minato. "We will continue tomorrow."

—

The next morning, when Kenji reached the dining room, Minato was already there having his breakfast.

"Good morning, Sensei," greeted Kenji. The sensei nodded in acknowledgment.

The participants took their seats. There was constant chatter in the room while they ate. After a while, they noticed Minato had not spoken a word. When they enquired, he said, "When you are hiking through a forest, be fully in the forest."

With that, he got up and walked towards the congregation hall. The participants understood, this was another sermon in mindfulness. A sermon where a lot was taught without a word being spoken. In those couple of days and during the following sessions, the participants were explained about mindfulness and various meditation techniques. Weekend after weekend, Kenji, along with others, returned to Kinkaku-ji to learn about techniques to know themselves better.

—

About three months later, Kenji alighted from the bus on a crisp winter morning. The hike no longer felt as tedious as it once did. Many participants visited regularly, though a few had dropped out. Kenji began the hike up to Kinkaku-ji. The air was fresh, cold, and clear. While climbing, he thought about the work accomplished during the week. Before his mind could focus on the future, the gurgling sound of a stream caught his attention. He took a detour to try and find it. It was almost sunrise as the birds started chirping. He took his phone out and began clicking pictures. He continued taking pictures throughout the hike. On Sunday morning, when Sensei Minato began his session, he noticed Kenji was missing. Kenji was present on Saturday and had never missed a session, so Minato was concerned.

"Does anyone know where Kenji is?" he asked the participants.

"Sensei, I saw him walking towards the stream this morning," replied one of them.

Minato asked another monk to conduct the class that day while he went to look for Kenji.

—

After a few minutes of walking, Minato found Kenji sitting quietly beside the steadily flowing stream. Minato sat on a rock beside him.

"Sensei," said Kenji, and stood up.

"Sit down, my friend," said Minato. "What is it that bothers you?"

After a brief hesitation, Kenji dropped his inhibitions. "Don't get me wrong, but I feel I am not experiencing changes in myself as expected. I am not sure if I should continue to come here."

"What is it that you are expecting?" asked Minato.

"To have found inner peace. To have reignited the light within me, to know myself better!"

"Hmm," Minato said, staring at the stream. "This is a beautiful stream!"

"Yes, it is," replied Kenji, confused.

"I believe it becomes prettier further down," said Minato.

"Yes, I agree. Look here," said Kenji as he took his phone out. See these beautiful pictures I clicked on the way up!"

"Beautiful!" exclaimed Minato, looking at the pics. "I believe you managed to put your baggage down while hiking!"

Kenji remained quiet; he understood what Minato was trying to say.

"Do you see that tree fallen in the stream that's obstructing its flow?" said Minato, pointing to the tree.

"Yes, Sensei," replied Kenji.

"For the next few days, I want you to sit here and just observe it."

"That's it?"

"Yes," smiled Minato, "And trust the process."

—

Kenji did as he was instructed for almost a month. There was a spring in his step as he alighted from the bus that Saturday. He began the hike once again. Without taking pictures and without a thought or worry, he climbed up at a steady pace. He soaked in the bounty of nature. He took deep breaths to take in fresh oxygen, listened closely to the song of the birds, observed beautiful flowers, and gazed at the mesmerising morning sky. With a smile on his face, he reached the place where he was supposed to sit and observe. There, he realised something had changed; the tree had been washed away by the flowing water.

"It's gone, isn't it?" asked Minato as he approached from behind.

"Sensei," said Kenji and bowed. "Yes."

"Sit down," said Minato. "How was your hike this morning?"

"Oh, it was so beautiful...." Kenji stopped, and a smile appeared on his face.

"What is it?" asked Minato.

"When I was hiking through the forest, I was fully in the forest," replied Kenji.

A glow of joy appeared on Minato's face. "How did it feel?"

"It is the best feeling I have ever had, thank you."

"You're welcome. You noticed our tree is missing."

"Yes, Sensei. I guess it finally got washed away."

"Yes, finally. You see, Kenji, everything takes time. You must be patient. The water kept hitting against the tree, and the current wasn't strong enough to push it away at once. With resilience and persistent effort, it managed to clear the path. It took time, but it happened," explained Minato.

"Like my expectations of myself?"

"That is correct, Kenji," replied Minato. "You were expecting results too soon. Nothing ever happens instantly.

There is a reason why they say patience is a virtue."

—

"Destruction, though, happens instantly, doesn't it? I mean the tree fell in an instant, didn't it?" asked Kenji.

Minato smiled. "Everything happens over a course of time. The tree fell in a moment, but the events that brought that moment into being were taking place a long time before that. Maybe the tree was sick, maybe it faced too many storms, maybe its roots weakened due to some parasites, we don't know for sure. What we do know is that a moment when things happen is just where events of the past culminate, that's it."

Kenji sat quietly listening to the master.

"Do you remember the first hike, Kenji?"

"Yes, Sensei."

"Do you see a difference between your first hike and the one today?"

"Yes, Sensei. During the first one, I was there but not there. Today, I am fully here!"

"That is the power of practice and patience. You did not quit like others did, you trusted your sensei, and that resilience has paid rich dividends," said Minato.

Kenji stood up and bowed to Minato. "Sensei, I am grateful that you found me and guided me to the right path. I am indebted to you for life!"

"There is no debt here, I am just fulfilling my duty as a teacher. Come, my friend, you may now return to the class," said Minato as they started walking towards the congregation hall.

~

25

A Full Circle

~ Amit Suri

In his early twenties, Sourav had once stumbled upon a line in a weathered old diary at a neighbourhood pawnshop. Scribbled in faded ink on the inside cover, it read: *"Any pain, including that of others, is felt when we internalise it, and it can be relieved when we empathise enough."*

At the time, it struck him as philosophical fluff. He copied it into his journal anyway, a habit he had developed – collecting profound-sounding things he didn't fully understand. He figured some truths took their time. Some needed life to unfold, for them to bloom with meaning.

—

Back in the 1980s, when Calcutta was still Calcutta and not yet Kolkata, time moved to a slower rhythm. That city, with its trams, the clang of metal shutters, and the scent of mustard oil drifting from kitchens, often slipped into darkness by early evening. Power cuts were not an inconvenience; they were a routine.

It was in this humid darkness that Sourav's father, Bimal Roy, would return from work.

Asthmatic and breathless, Bimal would climb the wooden stairs with heavy steps. At the door, he would pause and knock thrice – a coded rhythm the children had grown up recognising.

His sister, Rupali, would run to the kitchen and bring back a glass of cold water from the fridge.

His brother, Kaushik, would grab a folded newspaper and fan at Bimal urgently.

Sourav, the youngest, had a different role. His job was to knead the tension out of his father's tired body. At first, he did it playfully, but slowly, over the years, the massage became a quiet ritual of care.

"Sourav," his father would groan, easing into the welcoming bed. "You've got magic in those fingers of yours."

Sourav would smile shyly, working his small palms over shoulders that felt like slabs of stone. "One day I'll be like you, Baba," he'd whisper under his breath.

And he meant it.

To the boy, his father, Bimal Roy, was a colossus. With his broad chest, muscular forearms, thick calves, and a voice that could fill a room without needing to shout, his father was a presence. He carried an aura that could charm at a gathering or silence a room in seconds.

Sourav had always assumed manhood would be a straightforward inheritance. That one day, he'd simply wake up with the same frame, the same strength, the same gravity. That he, too, would walk into a room and have it bend, slightly if not completely, in his favour.

—

But time and tide, have their own will.

Despite his best efforts – regular gym sessions, protein shakes, push-ups till his arms trembled – Sourav remained slim. "Wiry!" his mother would say, with affectionate resignation. His body, it turned out, had inherited different genes, and his aura, well, it formed in the mind rather than the body.

So he turned to books. To classrooms. To chalkboards and lectures, and papers filled with ideas. If he couldn't carry his father's frame, perhaps he could carry the family name forward in another way.

He found solace in academia, in recognition of a different kind. But every now and then, standing in front of a mirror, he would flex his arms and smile sheepishly at his own reflection.

"Still not Baba," he'd mutter, towel slung around his neck to give some gravitas to his persona.

Time passed.

Careers were built. Marriages happened. Children were born. Parents aged.

—

In the final stretch of his life, Bimal Roy became a hushed version of himself. His voice softened. His shoulders collapsed inward. The oxygen tube became his constant companion. The oxygen concentrator machine, placed beside his bed, hissed and hummed like a tired lullaby.

"Cold water?" Sourav had asked once, out of habit.

"Doctors have forbidden it," his mother replied quietly, eyes rimmed red.

His father sipped water from a cup with trembling hands, a straw between his lips. He no longer summoned anyone. The knocks were gone. So were the trams and power cuts. But the heaviness remained – this time, in the silence that filled the room.

Still, some habits refused to die.

"Sourav," his father whispered one afternoon, barely audible over the oxygen flow, "will you...?"

Sourav nodded, not waiting for the rest. He pulled up the stool, sat by his father's side, and began massaging – shoulders, back, calves, feet – the same familiar route, now a map of memories.

Only now, there was no strength to knead. His father's skin hung loose, thin as paper. The muscles he once marvelled at were gone. He pressed lightly, afraid he might cause more pain than pleasure.

After two minutes, Bimal flinched. "Enough," he said. "That's enough."

Sourav pulled his hands back and sat quietly.

The silence lingered.

"Do you remember," his father asked suddenly, "those nights during power cuts?"

Sourav nodded. "Of course. You'd walk in like a storm, and we'd all jump into action."

His father chuckled. It was a dry, wheezing sound. "You always massaged very well."

"I liked touching your strength," Sourav said honestly.

There was a pause.

Then Bimal whispered, "Now you touch my skeleton."

Sourav looked away, eyes stinging.

It was in that moment that something shifted. That old quote, copied in youth without understanding, returned like a tide: *"Any pain, including that of others, is felt when we internalise it, and it can be relieved when we empathise enough."*

Now he understood. Deeply. Empathetically.

—

After Bimal's funeral, as the rituals concluded and relatives left with platitudes, Sourav stayed back. He lingered in the house longer than he'd planned, walking through rooms that still smelled faintly of eucalyptus oil and mothballs.

One evening, while sorting through drawers, he found a stack of old diaries. His father's handwriting, neat and assertive, sprawled across the pages. In one, dated 1984, a small note read:

"Sourav's hands... strong for such a little fellow. He'll grow into something fine. Maybe not like me, but in his own way."

Sourav closed the diary and wept.

—

A couple of years later, Sourav became a father himself. His son, Aryan, barely twelve, was helping him unpack boxes in their new flat in Pune.

"Dad," Aryan called out, holding up an old photo. "Who's this muscleman?"

Sourav looked over and smiled.

"That," he said, walking over, "was your grandfather."

"He looks like a superhero!"

"He was, in many ways."

Aryan looked at the photo again. "Will I look like him when I grow up?"

Sourav knelt, placed a hand on his son's shoulder. "Maybe. But whether or not you do, you'll find your own strength."

Aryan nodded thoughtfully. "You don't look like him, but you're strong too."

Sourav blinked, the words catching him off guard.

"Strong how?"

"You just are. I can feel it."

Sourav ruffled his son's hair. "That's the best compliment I've ever received."

—

And yet, on quiet nights, when the house slept, Sourav would sit by his window, cup of tea in hand, and wonder if time had really come full circle, or if it was merely an illusion created by memory and longing.

He missed the Calcutta of power cuts and folded newspapers. He missed the damp cottons of monsoon evenings, and his father's voice calling from the staircase.

He missed being a boy who thought strength was in muscle.

Time had moved, as tides do. And with it, it had taken away many things. But it had also returned something – the ability to feel another's pain – deeply, empathetically.

And that, he felt, was his greatest inheritance.

~

26

The Empty Nest

~ Kinjal Mehta

The elderly lady, Vaani, a 75-year-old woman with silver hair and a warm smile, took a few gentle steps to the park bench, her worn-out slippers making soft crunching sounds on the gravel path in the gardens of the ISKCON temple in Mumbai. She sat down, grateful for the chance to watch the sunrise and catch her breath and rest her tired legs. The winter sun cast a warm glow over her face, and she wrapped her dupatta tighter around her shoulders, feeling the soft fabric's comforting warmth of her salwar kameez. She placed her handbag neatly on her knee.

"Namaste," said the 78-year-old silver-haired gentleman, Veer, with a warm smile, as he folded his newspaper, the Times of India, at the other end of the bench.

"Beautiful morning, isn't it?"

Vaani smiled back, her eyes twinkling. "Yes, it is. The winter sun is just right." She adjusted her dupatta, her wrinkled hands fumbling with the soft fabric in the chilly air.

They sat in comfortable silence for a few moments, taking in the breathtaking view of the city, with the majestic Mahalaxmi Temple visible in the distance.

"I've always loved this view," Veer said, his eyes gazing out at the sprawling metropolis.

"Excuse me?"

"The view," Veer repeated, his eyes sparkling with nostalgia.

"I've been coming here since I was a *bachcha* (child). I used to watch the trains at Churchgate Station."

Vaani followed his gaze, down the hill towards the city, where the sounds of horns and chatter filled the air. "I loved the steam trains," Veer said wistfully. "Do you see the Western Railway line?"

Vaani nodded. "Yes, I can see. No more steam trains now, though, I'm afraid. Those were simpler times, when life moved at a slower pace."

Veer nodded in agreement. "It was. I'd travel across the country, attending music festivals and visiting relatives. My parents would worry about me, but I'd always manage to send them a postcard from somewhere." He chuckled. "Those were the days. Do you have any *santan* (children)?"

"Yes, two. And parampara (grandchildren) now, too," Vaani said, her eyes lighting up with pride.

"Then you're blessed. What are their names?" Veer asked, his eyes fixed on Vaani's gentle face, the long, white braid that rested over her shoulder.

"Naren, my beta (son), is the eldest. He has two little ones of his own now," Vaani said, beaming with pride. "Well, not so little now. They've grown and moved out, too. I don't get to see them as much as I'd like."

"I've always liked the name Naren," Veer said, smiling.

"And then there's Nalini, my beti (daughter). She got married, finally, last year. She's nearly fifty! She finally took the plunge and settled down," Vaani said, chuckling.

"Well, that's lovely!"

"It is. It was. She looked beautiful in her lehenga," Vaani said, her eyes shining with happiness.

Veer sat back, a wistful expression on his face. "I always wanted children of my own."

The silence between them was comfortable, like a warm cup of chai on a cold morning. Vaani broke the silence, "You can read your newspaper, Veer. I don't mind."

Veer smiled, "No, no, it's okay. I don't often get a chance to have a conversation with someone as lovely and beautiful as you." He said, with a gentle smile and a wink.

Vaani laughed and chuckled, "You're a charmer, aren't you? I bet you stole many hearts in your youth." Veer chuckled, "I don't know about that!" "Did you grow up around here, then?" Vaani asked, curiosity getting the better of her. "Yes," replied Veer. "Not far. And I went to school here, too. St. Xavier's... I think." He shook his head, "My memory isn't what it used to be."

"Age does that to us, doesn't it?" Vaani said, softly. Veer nodded, "I suppose it does."

She sighed, "It takes away the most precious things. Our *sharir* (body), our *mann* (mind), our *yaadein* (memories)."

The silence between them was palpable, as they gazed out at the cityscape, lost in their own thoughts.

Vaani broke the silence, "Veer, can I ask you something?"

He turned to her, his eyes warm and inviting. "Of course, Vaani-*ji*. Please ask."

"Have you ever been married?"

Veer shook his head, a hint of sadness in his eyes. "No, I never married. There was someone special, once... but that's all in the past now."

Vaani's eyes were filled with empathy. "I was fortunate enough to marry my best friend, my soulmate," she said, her voice barely above a whisper. "He was my everything."

Veer's face lit up with warmth. "That's wonderful!"

Vaani's eyes clouded over, "Yes, it was wonderful. But now he's gone, and I'm left with this terrible feeling of *shunya* (emptiness). It's a loneliness that's hard to describe." Vaani looked down at her lap, her eyes welling up with tears.

Veer's eyes filled with compassion as he took Vaani's hand in his "I'm deeply sorry for your loss. How long ago did he pass away?" Vaani's voice trembled,

"Around seven years ago. Nothing has been the same since." Tears welled up in her eyes, which had once shone bright like the stars on a clear night. Now, they seemed dull, like the moon during a lunar eclipse.

Veer's face was etched with concern. "That's a great loss. Do you have anyone close to you?" Vaani shook her head, "My children are busy with their own lives. Naren is in Bangalore, and Nalini is in Hyderabad. I feel like I'm just going through the motions, crossing names off my address book one by one." She paused, her voice cracking. "All my friends... they're all gone now."

Veer pulled out a handkerchief from his pocket and offered it to her. "It's okay, Vaani-*ji*. You're not alone."

Vaani smiled weakly, "Thank you." She wiped her eyes, "I'm so silly. You must think I'm an old woman, crying on a bench like this."

Veer's expression was gentle, "Not at all, Vaani-*ji*. You're just being human."

“Well, I feel like an old fool. I should be glad for what I have. I’m still here, my children are happy and healthy. You were right, I have been blessed.”

Veer looked puzzled. “What?”

“A minute ago, you said I was blessed. For having my children.”

“Oh, that’s right.” He shook his head. “I’m more forgetful the older I get.”

Vaani tried to return the handkerchief, but Veer refused, "Keep it, I have plenty. Consider it a small gift from me to you."

"Okay, I will. Thank you," Vaani said, tucking the handkerchief into her handbag and snapping it shut.

"*Zindagi* (life) is indeed a mystery, Veer," she said, her eyes gazing into the distance. "Isn't it?"

Veer tilted his head, not quite understanding. "In what way?"

Vaani's voice was tinged with melancholy, "I just... can't believe I'm here, at the twilight of my life. And what do I really have to show for it? Just a few memories, some faded photographs, and a handful of stories to tell."

Veer didn't reply, his face a picture of compassion. Vaani continued, "I don't feel any different than I did ten years ago.

Twenty years ago, even. But when I look in the mirror, an old woman looks back, with wrinkles and grey hair." She sighed, "It all feels so... *vyarth* (futile)."

Veer cleared his throat, "I'm not sure I can offer any answers, Vaani-*ji*. I'm afraid I'm still figuring out life myself." Vaani smiled weakly, "I know, Veer. I don't expect answers. I just needed to share my thoughts with someone."

The silence that followed was comfortable, like a warm blanket on a chilly evening.

Veer broke the silence, "I used to travel by train, you know. All around the country, from Kashmir to Kanyakumari."

"I think you mentioned that earlier." Vaani smiled,

Veer laughed, "I did?".

Vaani smiled indulgently. "Yes, and your parents would worry sick about you, not knowing where you were or when you'd return."

Veer chuckled, "Not like today, when we have mobile phones and GPS." Vaani nodded, "No, Veer. Life was simpler, yet more complicated, back then."

Veer looked at Vaani, his eyes searching. "You seem really familiar. Have we met before?"

Vaani's eyes filled with a mix of sadness and love. "Yes, Veer, we've met. We're married, remember?"

Veer's frown deepened. "Married?" Vaani nodded gently. "Yes, sweetheart. We've been married for many years. And now, it's time for us to head home. The cold is getting to me, and I have some hot chai ready for us."

Veer looked uncertain, but Vaani's gentle guidance helped him stand up. "Come on, Veer. Let's go home. We can watch the Formula 1 racing on TV, and then I'll make us some dinner."

As they walked hand in hand, Vaani thought about their

empty nest, their children grown and moved out, living their own lives in different cities. She smiled softly, remembering the happy times they had shared as a family.

"Don't forget your newspaper, Veer," she reminded him gently.

Together, they walked away from the park bench where they had sat every Sunday morning for the past few decades, their hands entwined, their love for each other still strong despite the challenges they faced, back to the home where they had raised their children. "Empty now," thought Vaani as she led her husband back through the park, "Entirely Empty."

~

27

In Her Own Time

~ Dr. Ekta Bhatia

Time, in my life, has always moved in measured milestones. It ticked in developmental charts, in therapy sessions marked by weekly progress. Tides came too as waves of emotions, struggle, hope, resilience - but I learned to ride those waves with professional poise.

For over two decades, as a therapist, I lived in that rhythm. From newborns to 90-year-olds, I held hands that shook, stumbled, and healed. Each hand had its own story - tiny fingers curling instinctively, aged palms lined with decades of living, trembling grips learning to trust again.

I thought I understood how time moved. I thought I understood the tides.

Until I met my daughter.

Over the years, I had walked beside hundreds of families, living through their joys and grief, silently gathering the wisdom of their mistakes and triumphs. Each of them shaped me. I believed I was growing wiser with each life I touched, collecting lessons I could one day pass on to my own children. But there was a shadow side to this gift. The more I saw, the more I preempted. I became someone who was always braced. Watching. Anticipating. At the time, I didn't realise how this quiet anxiety had seeped into my being until the moment

Meherr was born.

She arrived in the middle of a global pause. A COVID baby. The hospital corridors were empty of visitors, the world hushed by masks and caution. When she was finally brought to me, I was still reeling from the anesthesia. I couldn't hold her. My husband did, bringing her close enough for me to see. I had waited for this moment for years. I had imagined I would be overcome by that miraculous sense of arrival.

And yet.

The first thing I saw was her fingers.

Two thumbs.

A common variation. Nothing that required panic. But in my therapists' eyes, even small deviations were registered.

Something I had seen before, in therapy rooms where I was trained to look for every detail. And in that meeting with my daughter, that reflex, that lens did not leave me.

I had trained myself to be alert – to read bodies like stories, find signs before they became symptoms. But here, in my daughter's body, that vigilance felt like a betrayal. I wasn't meeting her – I was scanning her.

I couldn't speak. I tried to gesture, to tell my husband what I was seeing, but no words would come. Later, when he asked me what I had been trying to say, I began to cry.

"I should have seen her face," I said. "But I saw her fingers."

It wasn't grief, not fear, nor disappointment. It was a deep realization that I had seen her not as a mother first but as a therapist. That even in my most personal moment, I had led with professional instinct.

That realization washed over me like a tide.

I wasn't crying because something was wrong with her. I was crying because something had shifted in me. And I wasn't ready for it.

Time from that point on stopped being something I tracked. It became something I felt.

Meherr challenged more than just my understanding of time. She challenged my relationship with certainty. She didn't fit the patterns I had memorized.

And for the first time, I felt unsure. Not professionally, but personally.

The tools I had relied on for years suddenly felt too sharp. The timelines are too tight. The labels were too loud.

I had trained myself to pick patterns. But with her, I had to learn to pause before placing meaning. To allow space without rushing to fill it.

She was teaching me something I hadn't mastered in all my years of practice...

To wait.

To witness.

To trust.

It wasn't easy. It still isn't.

I had spent a lifetime intervening, solving, guiding. It took effort to hold back that impulse.

But in the quiet hours of watching her play, explore, hesitate, and retreat, I began to unlearn.

Unlearn the need to fix.

Unlearn the habit to name.

Unlearn that reflex to lead.

She taught me to slow down. To soften. To see her as she was, not as she could be.

And in doing so, she gave me a new rhythm – one that didn't follow charts or checklists, but moved like the tide – gentle, sure, and uniquely her own.

Twenty years of work gave me a map. But motherhood taught me that sometimes, you must walk without one. That presence matters more than prediction.

The therapist in me still notices. Still cares. Still watches. But the mother in me now waits.

Waits for time to do its work. Waits for tides to wash gently.

This is the balance I have found. In the space between knowing and feeling, between fear and surrender, between time and tide – I am becoming.

And so is she.

She is not just becoming who she is meant to be – she is also shaping who I am still learning to become.

~

28

Rays of Renewal

~ Saloni Chheda

"I can't do it anymore, Mummy. I'm leaving for Mumbai today." Payal stood with her bags, wearing a red satin top and blue denim jeans, hoping desperately that her mother, Anita, would come with her.

"I've done everything I could, Ma. I've told the maid everything about your medicine. She'll be here twenty-four hours a day in case you need anything." Payal's voice wavered slightly as she took her mother's blessings. "Goodbye, Mummy."

With that, she left the room.

Anita, who was completely bedridden with arthritis, was shocked to see her daughter leaving. Tears rolled down her cheeks as she wept uncontrollably. After all, Payal was her only hope following her husband's tragic death.

Anita had been married to Ashok Mehta, a well-known businessman of Ahmedabad and a self-made millionaire. His rise to success had been a story of grit, determination, and strategic brilliance. He'd loved his wife and daughter more than anything in the world. At the age of fifty-five, Ashok had suffered a massive heart attack, bringing a tragic end to his remarkable life.

Anita herself had been a teacher, highly respected amongst her colleagues. She was warm and exceptionally patient, often offering guidance and creating a nurturing environment where students felt free to express themselves. She'd possessed grace in every wrinkle and had glowed radiantly at the age of fifty-two. She'd worn crisp linen saris, pleated perfectly, with a red rose tucked into her hair and a large bindi adorning her forehead, which added elegance to her appearance.

Nothing had stopped her from going to school, not even when she'd discovered her arthritis condition. She'd been determined, doing her exercises and physiotherapy sessions religiously to prevent the swelling in her legs and hands, knowing that neglecting them might lead to serious consequences.

It was only when the devastating news of her husband's death reached her that she crumbled completely. For her, the world seemed to tilt, and time slowed to a crawl. The room, once familiar and comforting, now felt distant, as if life itself had stepped away, leaving her stranded in the aftermath of profound loss. She would lie in bed, gazing endlessly through the window. Seasons changed, but nothing seemed to move her anymore.

Her daughter Payal had remained by her side during these difficult times. Payal had been in her final year of law college in Ahmedabad when her father passed away. She possessed a mixture of determination, intellectual curiosity, and ambition, just like her father. She'd managed her studies and the household admirably. Every day, she'd accompany her mother to physiotherapy sessions, but Anita would somehow skip some of them, resulting in stiffness in her fingers and swollen legs. After several months, Anita simply stopped attending altogether, rendering her completely bedridden.

After Payal's final year examinations, she was selected for a position as a litigator at a Mumbai-based firm. She was tremendously excited about the opportunity, but she couldn't possibly leave her mother in such a condition. Payal knew her mother needed her more than ever. She would repeatedly urge her mother to accompany her to Mumbai, but Anita refused every single time.

One day, Payal was particularly firm in her approach.

"Mummy, could we please go to Mumbai together? I must take this job, and I'd love it if you could come and stay with me there," Payal pleaded earnestly.

"I'm sorry, dear, but I don't wish to leave this house or travel anywhere," Anita replied in a sluggish tone, dismissing her daughter's wishes entirely.

Payal grew upset. "Why are you doing this to yourself, and to me? I've been waiting ages for this opportunity to go to Mumbai, and you're rejecting me just to stay here. I'm asking for one small favour from you. Why can't you come and live with me? If you did, I could take proper care of you in Mumbai. Please try to understand."

"You may go," Anita replied flatly, "but I'm staying here."

"Mummy, you're being completely irrational! You know perfectly well I can't leave you here alone."

Anita remained silent and simply turned to the other side of the bed. Payal stormed out angrily and went to her own room.

It was autumn, when sunlight filtered softly through amber leaves. Anita waited eagerly for her daughter, believing everything would somehow be fine. But to her shock, Payal appeared with two bags of luggage and departed without another word.

Anita lay in her bed, stunned and trying to process what had just happened, weeping continuously. Initially, she felt angry with her daughter: "How could she leave me in this situation? Do I matter less than her job? Her father left us with such wealth that she doesn't even need to work. How can I possibly live without her? I need her every morning to help me eat. How could she be so heartless? Now the maid will have to feed me, I don't want that. She doesn't realise how swollen my feet and hands are. How can I manage without her?"

After repeated attempts to call, Payal wouldn't answer. Anita lay on her bed, feeling utterly helpless.

As the days passed, Anita's thoughts began to shift: "What a dreadful mother I am. How could I do this to my child? My daughter has been doing so much for me. Why can't I be with her? How could I be so unreasonable?"

Anita made up her mind, determined to begin exercising and attending physiotherapy again. A new ray of hope emerged, soft yet certain, like the first light after a long storm. She was once again filled with purpose in her life – a purpose so strong it surged within her, unstoppable and unwavering.

Anita arranged for her physiotherapist to visit her at home for several days to establish a rhythm of movement. She was once again filled with joy, pride shining through her tears, and a never-give-up attitude that kept her progressing. Gradually, her condition improved, though she never told her daughter about her efforts. Anita kept her calls to Payal brief and shared only minimal details.

After three to four months of rigorous exercise and unwavering determination, the doctors were delighted to see Anita's improvement and gave her clearance to travel. Anita had tears in her eyes, knowing she would see her daughter again after four long months.

It was nearly December when Anita decided to surprise Payal. She booked her flight ticket and packed her bags, filled with confidence and rays of renewal. December in Mumbai is misty, with a tender chill in the air. Anita arrived on a Sunday morning, knowing it was Payal's holiday, and rang the doorbell. She was nervous yet thrilled to see her daughter's reaction.

"Surprise!" Anita exclaimed, beaming at her daughter.

"Mummy, you came!" Payal gasped, unable to believe her eyes. "How? When? What?" she asked excitedly, tears streaming down her cheeks.

She had countless questions for her mother. Anita embraced her daughter tightly and kissed her forehead tenderly.

"I've come to stay with you now, darling," Anita explained everything that had transpired. "I can't bear to be apart from you."

Payal's eyes shone with pride as she struggled to control her tears of joy.

Several years later, Payal was cheering enthusiastically for Anita with every step she took during a marathon race in Mumbai.

"You've got this, Mummy!" she shouted, clapping and waving signs filled with love and motivation. "Keep going!"

Anita, with her purpose burning so strongly within her, had transformed every obstacle into a stepping stone, making each moment feel alive with promise. She was reminded that even after the darkest nights, the sun never fails to rise and shine again.

~

29

The Screen Between Us

~ Manasvi Mehta

2037. The year I finally looked up.

My name, Mira, blinked across the inside of my AI glasses, the soft pulse nudging me toward the Therapy Room. I hated that feeling – like the world was always watching, always prompting, always reminding me who I was supposed to be.

I didn't want to be here.

"I don't belong in therapy," I whispered to myself. "I'm fine. Someone, just get me out of this place."

But I wasn't fine. I was twenty-two, and I had been unraveling for years – anxiety, depression, and a digital addiction so deep it felt like part of my DNA. Not to substances but to screens. To the curated version of myself, I'd been performing since I was four.

My mother, Vanika, sat outside the therapy center, her own glasses dimmed to privacy mode. She'd lost her job to AI last year. Strategic planning has been replaced by predictive algorithms. That loss had forced her to see me clearly for the first time in years. And what she saw terrified her.

My mother always meant well. She was dedicated, relentless even, in her pursuit to give me the best life possible. But somewhere along the way, her efforts to keep me sharp, to keep me ahead, backfired.

Now, when I look back, it's staggering how fast the years have passed. Seventeen years since the virus swept across the planet and locked us all inside. Seventeen years since the world shifted from touch to screen, from presence to projection.

And yet, today – March 2037 – feels like time has just ticked its way out. Like the clock has finally stopped pretending it's on our side.

The therapy room adjusted to my biometric readings as I stepped inside. Temperature, lighting, even scent – everything calibrated to soothe me. But I didn't want 'comfort'. I wanted 'escape'.

Nina greeted me with a soft smile. She always did. She never pushed, never judged. Just listened.

"Mira," she said, "I'm glad you're here. Can you tell me about your childhood?"

I hesitated. Then I let the memories surface.

Navigating through my childhood, I reflected, thinking, who introduced me to this? Were they my friends around me, or was it my mother who was equally addicted to the cell phone as I grew up, following in her footsteps?

Nina, my therapist, was keen on listening, and as I started narrating, a mixture of joyous and bitter moments flashed across me

Mira: I was just 5 years old. My vivid and joyful memories of celebrating my birthday were filled with lots of anxiety and anticipation of how things would turn out. My parents were surely much more excited about the entire event, as this was their way of socializing with people around, most of them with whom we are not in touch.

And suddenly, a pandemic lockdown changed everything around us. My birthday was surely cancelled, but that didn't affect me much, unlike my parents. But what affected us changed our lives forever. Schools were suddenly shut, my parents started working from home, and looking at them all the time was something that I had secretly prayed for. My excitement was palpable as I felt more comfortable and secure with everyone around me.

My parents had high aspirations for my success and wanted to provide me with every opportunity to excel. In their efforts to give me the best even in this situation of lockdown, they inadvertently created a packed schedule, throwing me into the digital world that left me with little downtime. That was the end of my childhood at the age of 5.

I was innocent when I came across the cell phone.

The world around us, due to lockdown, trapped us all and confined us into this digital world that made me and everyone around me... slaves.

I was addicted to the world of fake gratitude, where being happy was only by showing digitally I was happy.

I was introduced to the screen at the age of 4, which gulped me in very deeply that today I need help to sustain and survive mentally.

I could not start my day without looking at my cell phone.

Nina: Yes, Mira, your dependence on your digital aid has slowly pulled you in. Please, can you share more about your days in school?

I smiled because what were supposed to be days of fun,

playing with friends and running around in the garden, I was only scrolling some reels, which made no sense, but subconsciously made me mirror my behaviour most aggressively.

Today, sitting in this therapy center, who do I blame? My parents, who had to forcefully introduce me to the screen for the online classes as education was more important than anything, or the peer pressure my parents faced in maintaining their own goals, careers, and social life.

As time passed, things around me changed, but one thing remained constant, and that was the world of being digitally active. When I was 8 years old, first my grades fell, then my attitude changed.

My teacher wanted to see my mother, but I snapped back. I gave her a look, something I felt was copied from the constant videos on the cell phone I was looking at. Slowly, I started changing, something my parents could have stopped, but maybe they were preoccupied with their lives, leaving very little time for me. I started having disturbed sleep, cognitively I started becoming slower, and even the slightest of advice given to me would leave me in an aggressive mood.

The vicious cycle continued with everyone around me just to make me do the basic activities of life.

Not brushing – *I was given the phone!*

Not eating the right food – *I was given the phone!*

Not letting my mother do her office work – *I was given the phone!*

Not sitting in a restaurant quietly – I was given the phone!

And then my mother realized something was wrong, so

suddenly she took away the screen from me, leaving me more combative. But she was not that stern enough to live up to her own actions, and within two days, I would get my screen back.

Why wouldn't I get it back? Was I addicted? No, it was my mother who was addicted.

She couldn't leave her digital world and give me some time just to play with her. Her interactions were limited to my education, my classes, and how well I could perform everywhere.

My mother's confidence was raised depending on everyone's gratification she would receive through her social media, where everyone would praise her for how well she was raising me. Naturally, I was mimicking her style, where my approach to doing anything was only to end it by uploading it on social media.

Mom could have stopped. She didn't, so I couldn't stop my screen time either!

Nina stopped me in between and handed me a glass of water. She was introspecting the truth, who was I blaming?

Nina: Are you blaming your mother? You did not understand what was right at that time, but today you do know how you can keep your self-control. She did what seemed to be an easier way out, but you are again following in her footsteps by taking the easy way and not leaving the digital world.

But Nina, I cannot stop! I have tried multiple times where I would uninstall my apps, I would try to meditate, but in the end, I have this strong urge to know about what is happening in everyone's life.

There have been days when I have forgotten to take a

shower, brush my teeth, and even skipped a meal, as my focus is only on the digital world, where I am constantly looking for gratitude. My entire day goes bad if my friends around me have failed to respond on social media. I get affected seeing what they are doing, where they are travelling, and I try to show them that I am no less.

But Nina, the truth is I am not happy, I am crying every night. Am I actually getting into depression at this age due to my addiction to the phone?

Nina: YES, but rather than focusing on what is already spoiled, can we work on how we reverse the entire problem?

Will it be possible for you to connect with 3 friends over coffee? You have many friends right over your social page?

Also, can you share a few stories about your teenage days when you come to me?"

I tried to contact one friend of mine the next day. Just within a few minutes, I realized I had nothing to talk about as my awkwardness kept increasing about how I could be myself in front of anyone. This small task just made me accept how distant I had grown from everyone and how difficult it was for me to maintain contact with everyone on a personal level rather than a digital one. Maybe I realized having people around was more important rather than having so many friends over a social account.

—

On my next visit, I was more excited...

Nina: Hi Mira, Good to see this smile on your face. I see it is not only your smile, but you are maintaining more eye contact with me, which is a very good sign.

Just then, I realized how I was perpetually avoiding people around me, and my parents would have surely shared with Nina how I was unable to communicate with them.

Mira: So Nina, let me share my teenage days. They were considered one of the best days for me but somewhere I have had a mixture of emotions rolling over me.

I was just 13 years just when I hit puberty, I counted myself as an adult now, though no one agrees to this. My only wish was to have my own social identity. I had now accepted that if I wanted to be known, I needed to show everything.

My mother wasn't ready to give me the cell phone, but with all my convincing capacity, she finally gave in, and I had my own cell phone.

I wish she could have stopped me that time!

I wouldn't have uploaded all my pictures in this fake world, where I too had started looking out for gratitude and praises of how good I looked.

I could have stopped. I didn't, as I had subconsciously trained myself to raise my confidence by just showing off the entire world how fake smiles work, even though one is not smiling.

I was slowly slipping into anxiety.

Nina: Ok, maybe your mother was trying to give you that freedom, which, in case she had not given you, you would have accused her of being bossy over you. As a mother, she herself was scared and unsure as she could clearly see how much you were getting into the digital world, but when she could see you academically doing well, she was not concerned, as the future was bleak for her too.

Mira, today you know what is right and wrong, you are mature enough to make your own decisions, and the biggest change is that you have accepted to take help from us for your addiction; you are sure to do well in your future life.

I know this is one of the most challenging tasks, but could you initiate going for lunch with your parents, definitely keeping the phone in your bag all throughout the time when they are with you.

Nina, this is difficult! My tone suddenly changed. Friends are easy, Nina.

Friends are my age, but parents, I just can't talk to my mother even for the slightest of things going around.

How can I spend two hours of lunchtime with them? Nina, I feel they don't understand me at all. I cried.

"Can you try? Just once," Nina requested me.

Ok, as I have no choice but to trust my friends is easier than trusting my parents. I told her, making my way towards the exit and thinking about how I would go ahead with this meeting.

I had no choice but to initiate this outing with my parents. It is just a task, and it shall get over, I told myself.

Surprisingly, my parents understood me more this time in my selection of places, where we would go, and what we would do. Maybe that time I realized they were getting old, too. They were no longer my parents who wanted to dictate over my life; in fact, they just wished to be a part of my world, where they were always there to support me more than my friends.

—

My next visit with Nina was the last one

Nina: Hey Mira, happy to see your mother coming along with you today. Since you know this is the last session, do you remember why you were brought here?

Yes, Nina, I came to you a year back, just as I couldn't finish my graduation in college. I was detained for being aggressive, and I could not stand anyone around me.

Nina knew that two years back, my life revolved only around digital aid. I had stopped communicating with everyone around me. My behavior tagged me that I needed to seek help. I had snapped at my colleague, thrown a fit towards my parents by throwing off my plate from the table, and locked myself up. Isn't this ok? I apologized and regretted it but somewhere everything around me got over my nerves. I got frustrated at the slightest change, and my parents claimed

I didn't talk to them, and I communicated with them only through the phone!

But did they talk to me when I was young? They would only respond by looking at their cell phones. Honestly, I hated being around my parents as I only felt they couldn't understand me. I felt I was closer to my friends than my parents.

I knew I was addicted, but every morning I woke up, I needed to look at my phone. I had a panic attack when I couldn't find my phone for an hour, only to find it below my bed. I knew it was bad, but it gave me security and closeness in a world where no one could enter.

But today I felt better, as I know where I needed to stop myself. I silently thanked my mother for getting me here and guiding me to seek help.

I hugged Nina and left.

—

VANIKA (Mira's Mother)

Time has passed, and I cannot go back. I saw Mira talking to herself when she couldn't go for a trip with her friends, as they felt she didn't fit in. Slowly, as I connected the dots, I realized my daughter was lost deep into her own world where she could confine her thoughts and feelings with strangers.

She stopped making eye contact with me as she grew older, only for me to realize she was losing her own self. I knew she needed help as her addiction to the screen increased, compromising her health and progress.

I wish I had not introduced her to this digital world. I wish I had spent more time with her, because it's said time waits for no one, so we should always try to make the best out of it.

Time doesn't wait for anyone, but if I get a chance to go back, I would just stop the screen and invest my time in her childhood, which I took away from her.

~

30

Reunion

~ Jay Solanki

In this digital age, keeping in touch with old friends is remarkably easy. I find myself in numerous WhatsApp groups – school batchmates, junior college friends, engineering colleagues, certificate course companions, first job associates, coaching class alumni, and even bus buddies. It's amusing how we end up hyper-interacting with people we'd barely known at school, or those who'd hardly acknowledged our presence back then. Now we share jokes, memories, life updates, and political leanings with complete abandon. Who would have thought?

It all began with Orkut – remember that dinosaur? That clunky yet lovable site warmed everyone up for Facebook, which later sparked the movement known as "Reunion." Then came BBM, followed by WhatsApp groups, which have become the unofficial archive of our shared pasts.

Thanks to technology, lost connections have been brought back to life. However, this story isn't about me. It's about my seventy-eight-year-old mother and a friendship that blossomed in the quiet streets of Pune during the 1960s.

She attended M. N. Shah School* near Bhopla Chowk in the Camp area. One of her fondest memories is of a girl named Fatima*. Their bond was warm and joyful – they rushed through lunch to squeeze in extra playtime during breaks, moving between each other's homes like sisters separated only by walls. Fatima was more than a friend; she was a key figure in every childhood story my mother shared.

"Do you remember when we used to race to finish our tiffins?" my mother would say during family carrom games, her eyes sparkling. "Fatima was always faster, but she'd wait for me anyway."

But life took its own course. The last time they met was at Fatima's wedding, right after my mother had married. Without landlines or other ways to keep in touch, their friendship quietly faded away. Years later, when my parents visited Pune to find Fatima's family, they discovered nothing – the house had changed hands long ago.

Over the years, I often heard my mother wonder aloud, "What must Fatima be doing now?" It was less a question and more a wistful sigh. At her age, one simply hopes childhood friends are still alive and keeping well.

Then came 2014 – the year a Google TV advert touched the nation. It featured two childhood friends separated by the partition, reunited by their grandchildren through a Google search. I showed it to my mother.

She teared up and softly asked, "Do you think we can find Fatima?"

Honestly, I'd never thought of it before. But seeing her reaction sparked something within me. There's something profoundly human about watching one's parents reconnect with their childhood – we want to glimpse what their world looked like. One way is to see them interact with childhood friends. It feels like time turning back, if only for a moment.

So I did what any modern detective would do – I googled Fatima's surname, Karjatwala*. Unfortunately, I found nothing. A few years passed, then one idle evening, I typed "Fatima Karjatwala" into Facebook. Again, nothing. I even messaged a random uncle I'd found with the same surname. No response.

Then the pandemic hit – a pause in our lives. In years to come, the global timeline will split into two eras: B.C. and A.P. – Before Covid and After Pandemic. The virus changed everything, taking young lives and leaving the elderly feeling like survivors on a deserted shore.

My parents survived, thankfully. But during those long lockdown months, their conversations grew heavier. They began naming peers who had passed away. My mother became quieter.

One day, she softly said, "I don't think I shall ever see Fatima again."

That night, I went to LinkedIn – a platform meant for professional networking. I typed in "Karjatwala" and stumbled upon one Mr. Farzan Karjatwala*. Using a trial of LinkedIn Premium – a digital VIP pass allowing me to contact strangers – I messaged him, explaining that I was searching for a woman named Fatima Karjatwala. I didn't expect much; it was a common name amongst Muslims.

A day later, Farzan replied: "Fatima is my aunt."

I shared more details – the school she'd attended in Pune. Farzan responded that he'd check with her son. That very day, I received the message: "Yes, she's the same Fatima, and she remembers your mother."

I rushed to tell my mother. She froze, eyes wide, hands trembling slightly. In that moment, she wasn't seventy-eight – she was a girl again, waiting to hear from her best friend at the school gate.

Soon, I obtained Fatima's son's number. That evening, my phone rang. A gentle, emotional voice asked, "May I speak with your mother, please?"

I handed her the phone. What happened next was a conversation through a time machine. Two twelve-year-old girls were having a blast on the telephone.

"Fatima! Is it really you?" my mother exclaimed.

"My darling friend! I've thought of you so many times over the years!"

They burst into laughter, tears, and memories. They video-called each other, and I swear the air shimmered with nostalgia. Fatima aunty couldn't stop blessing me.

"You're an angel, beta," she kept saying. "An absolute angel."

All I'd done was punch a few words on a keyboard, uniting two friends after fifty long years.

Since then, they've been inseparable – at least online – with 'Good Morning' messages, flower GIFs, lengthy chats with voice notes, and video calls. Then came a significant day: Fatima Aunty's granddaughter was getting married. My mother attended the wedding in Pune.

It was a grand reunion. Their warm embrace stole the show, overshadowing even the newlyweds on stage. Some guests showered them with flowers. There wasn't a dry eye in the room.

"Look at them," one guest whispered. "Fifty years melted away in an instant."

What seemed impossible became possible through technology. But more importantly, it happened through love. We often value technology and use relationships. Perhaps it's time we reversed that – let's use technology and value human relations instead.

As I watched my mother's face light up during her daily calls with Fatima, I realised I'd given her something priceless: the gift of yesterday, wrapped in the possibilities of today.

* *While this is a true lived story, the names have been changed to protect the individuals' identities.*

~

31

The Window Seat

~ Payal Shah

The first time Naina slammed the door, she had successfully stepped into her teenage era.

Not in anger – not really. More like protest theatre. The kind of exaggerated defiance that said, I'm mad, but also watching to see if you care.

I stood outside her room for a full minute, unable to move, holding a kerchief, wondering when my little girl, who once found joy in making friendship bracelets out of shoelaces, had turned into this hormonal storm cloud. I couldn't believe my eyes had just witnessed a teenager coming into being, a glimpse of my next couple of years.

"She's at that age," my neighbour offered helpfully, as though 'that age' was a valid reason for the chaos she now brought into our lives.

But it wasn't just her age. It was her spirit, like her personality was taking a 360-degree turn. She had questions about everything: school uniforms, family WhatsApp groups, and why I insisted on oiling her hair every Sunday.

And I, Meera Deshpande, the logic and list expert, was baffled.

—

I tried parenting like I managed my pantry: neatly labelled

rules, regular top-ups of discipline, and the occasional sweet treat for encouragement.

But Naina wasn't a shelf I could organise.

She stormed out of the kitchen one day because I refused to let her wear ripped jeans to a family lunch.

"This is my body, Ma! I'm not asking to pierce my nose!" she yelled as it was her right to do so, as if she was doing me a favour by not piercing her nose.

I blinked. "You're thirteen!" I followed her.

She crossed her arms. "Exactly. I'm not eight. Stop treating me like a project."

That night, I cried into the sink while washing dishes. Not because she had spoken rudely. But because, deep down, I feared she was right.

—

She called my world "boxed" one evening.

"Everything about you is... so boxed, neatly arranged, Ma. You wake up, make tea, go to work, come home, watch the news, sleep; it is like you have turned into a robot. You never colour outside the lines."

"Because I have responsibilities," I snapped.

She shrugged. "And I have dreams. Guess... we're both stubborn."

For a second, I saw myself in her – the younger me who once wanted to become a writer, not a bank officer. But I had folded those dreams neatly into files labelled "practical."

And here was my daughter, refusing to fold anything.

—

She started journaling around the same time – scribbling furiously into a purple notebook that she guarded like state secrets.

One day, she forgot it on the dining table.

I didn't mean to open it.

Okay, I did.

But only one page.

The entry read:

"Ma has made it her life's mission to make my life miserable, to boss me around. Her life revolves around me and my life; it is suffocating. She just doesn't get it. But I think she used to. She just forgot how to feel big feelings. I think adults trade their 'whys' for 'what ifs'. I won't. Not yet."

I put the notebook down, stunned.

—

Things didn't magically change after that. There were still slammed doors, silent dinners, and eye-rolls. But I began listening. Not just to her, but to myself. I started to respond to her wishes and requests instead of reacting dramatically to them.

I stopped saying, "You'll understand when you're older."

I started saying, "Help me understand now."

Slowly, she stopped seeing me as the villain in every scene. I stopped needing to be the hero.

We met somewhere in the middle: the messy, magical, maddening space between mother and almost-woman.

—

One rainy Sunday, I found her curled up by the window seat, her favourite spot, especially during storms.

"Can I sit with you?" I asked.

She looked up, surprised. "You hate rain."

"I'm trying new things."

She smiled and enthusiastically made room for me, "Character development. We love to see it."

We sat in silence, watching the world turn wet and wild. She held my hand without words.

And I realised that raising Naina wasn't about controlling her – it was about unfolding with her.

She wasn't becoming despite me.

She was becoming beside me.

~

32

Myrna and the River of Change

~ Vijay Lalla

Myrna Lalla leaned out of the ferry, watching bundles of driftwood bob past, while the sun shimmered on the slow-moving waters of the Tapti River. Each piece was a story. A remnant of a flood, a broken part of a tree, or a memory of a storm. To others, it was debris. To her, it was destiny.

Myrna was eighteen, fresh out of school. That May morning, as she stepped onto the mud-streaked banks of Mandvi, a small village near Gujarat's western coastline, she wasn't the same girl who once walked the manicured corridors of her school alongside children of film stars and CEOs. She had changed. It all began on a charity trip organized by her school in Grade 12.

—

"Myrna, don't forget your sketchbook," her teacher, Ms. Fernandes, reminded her as their flight landed at Bhuj Airport in the great desert of Kutch, Gujarat.

"Yes, Ma'am!" Myrna beamed. She loved sketching. That trip would change her forever.

"We're visiting Shivran village," Ms. Fernandes announced. "Your task is simple: Observe. Understand. Empathize."

In that dusty, humble village near Mandvi, Myrna met Shivani.

Shivani was nine, bright-eyed, barefoot, and radiant. But her eyes carried more wisdom than most adults Myrna knew.

"Why don't you go to a better school?" Myrna asked gently as they sat beneath a neem tree.

"Papa says no English. No money," Shivani shrugged. "We work in fields. I want good shoes... books... like you." Almost throughout the day at the camp, Shivani followed Myrna like ducklings following their mother.

That night, Myrna cried silently under a mosquito net in her guesthouse. And something within her shifted. For the first time, her education had collided with real life. She didn't just want to be a designer. She wanted to be *useful*.

—

Myrna's first-year design project brief was: *Design for Social Impact*. Most of her classmates designed elegant metro benches, eco-friendly shopping bags, and city park furniture.

But Myrna had a vision. A rural furniture line made from compressed driftwood and harvest grass – lightweight, durable, modular – inspired by IKEA but rooted in India. Tools. Shelves. Study desks. Motivational quote posters engraved on recycled grass-wood. All were designed to be made by villagers.

She named the project: *Nadiyaan Crafts* – the name 'Nadiyaan' was inspired by the Tapti River.

—

The monsoon had just ended. Myrna arrived with three giant boxes, a file folder, a used laptop, and a printer. Her prototypes were all in place. SOPs translated to Gujarati. Her mind swirled with hope.

She stayed at a local dharamshala and arranged a meeting at the village chaupal.

Myrna: "I want to train five of you. Just five. I'll show you how to make things out of grass, mud, and driftwood. We'll sell it abroad. We'll use the river, the port."

Whispers and suspicion filled the air.

Farmer: "Export? From here?"

Old Woman: "Will the river really carry our dreams, beti?"

Myrna (smiling): "Yes, Maaji. It already carries our wood. Why not our hope?"

Five agreed. One of them was Rakesh, a 23-year-old whose father was once a bonded labourer. Rakesh had worked at Mundra Port and knew the export documentation process.

But trouble wasn't far behind.

—

A burly landlord who controlled half the village, Shambhu didn't like change. He especially didn't like city girls empowering his workers.

Shambhu: *"Export ka sapna dikha ke logon ko bhadka rahi hai.* This girl will leave, but my village will suffer."

He sent two of his men to Myrna's lodge. Dayabhai (Goon no 1) : "Pack your bags. This isn't your place."

But Shivani saw them.

She ran, barefoot, door to door.

Shivani: "Myrna Didi is in danger!"

Twenty children with whistles and sticks surrounded the goons.

Vidyut : "Leave her alone!"

Vasant : "She's helping us!"

A war of wills began.

—

Inside a small shed, the training began.

Rakesh: "First, collect driftwood from the river after monsoon. Next, dry and compress it with resin and fibers."

Myrna: "Use this mold to create desk panels. The poster designs are pre-carved. Just print and press."

The kids helped too. Shivani designed motivational quotes.

Shivani: "I want girls to read: '*I am not less.*'"

Myrna: "Beautiful. That goes on the first poster."

They raised Rs. 1000 each. Bought a second-hand laptop. A printer. Rakesh managed online tax registration. His friend from Mundra Port helped with customs.

The first shipment of 25 wooden toolkits and motivational posters left via the Tapti River on a barge. It reached Mundra Port in 2 days.

—

An SMS pinged.

Rakesh: "Money has come! Rs. 58,000!"

Shouts. Tears. Laughter.

A village that once whispered doubts now danced.

That night, under fairy lights, kids performed skits about rivers and driftwood. Women cooked for 200. Music blasted from old speakers.

And to everyone's surprise, Shambhu Bhai arrived.

Shambhu: "What I tried to stop... has brought smiles I hadn't seen in years. Forgive me."

Myrna walked up and held out a toolkit.

Myrna: "You can build too."

He took it.

—

Vijay Lalla sat by the window, watching the sea. He opened his laptop and began to type:

"My daughter, Myrna, is not just a design student.

She is a river of change.

Her school did not just teach her subjects.

It taught her spirit.

From Juhu to Mandvi, from driftwood to destiny, she crafted hope.

Not just for Shivani.

But for a generation."

—

Somewhere, a mother sits on a stone bench by the river. Her son reads the story aloud.

Son: "Mumma, can I be like Myrna one day?"

Mother (smiling, with tears): "Yes, beta. But remember, true education is not just about learning. It's about lifting."

And the river continues to carry dreams downstream.

~

33

A Gulmohar Childhood

~ Ami Dedhia

Some memories don't just linger – *they breathe*. They bloom quietly in our minds, wrapped in fragrance, sound, and speak of the rhythm of times gone by. These special memories typically revive for me with the scent of Raatrani, the quiet of candlelit dinners, and the rustle of red petals under a Gulmohar tree I once called mine.

I was just four when the tide turned.

The current of life swept us away from the comforting chaos of Mumbai – a joint family home filled with familiar smells, endless chatter, and warm hands – into the untouched wildness of Panchgani. My brother, two years older, clung tightly to the city he loved. I, too young to understand the weight of what we'd left behind, simply followed – wide-eyed, curious, and unaware that I was walking into a place that would define me.

This was 1984. Panchgani wasn't the charming hill station people rave about presently.

Back then, Panchgani was raw, rugged, and wrapped in silence – more forest than town. Tucked high in the Sahyadris, it was known as an educational hub, home to some of the country's oldest and most prestigious boarding schools. A few had even shaped the lives of celebrities, their ivy-covered walls echoing both academic discipline and sporting spirit. With over 3,000 students spread across 20 institutions, it was a town brimming with youthful energy – yet somehow, it never lost its stillness.

But to me, it wasn't an educational destination. It was a living storybook – a jungle with winding lanes, singing trees, and magic hidden in the mist. A place untouched by time, where childhood felt endless and nature was always just a step away.

The streets weren't paved with concrete. Instead, they wore canopies of Gulmohar and Silver Oak trees, their branches stretched out like royal archways. In summer, the Gulmohars would shed their fiery blossoms, carpeting the ground in red – a trail made for barefoot wanderers like me. Peacocks strutted through our garden. Foxes and hyenas weren't just stories in books – they often walked beside us on misty school mornings, as if they too were part of the morning routine. *Nature wasn't a backdrop. It was the entire script.*

We had traded skyscrapers for the towering Sahyadris, and traffic horns for the rhythmic ringing of church bells on crisp Sunday mornings. The Raatrani bushes perfumed the night air. Every corner of this new world held a different kind of silence – one that didn't feel empty but full – full of whispers, of stillness, of soul.

As the years passed, Panchgani became home.

The tides of time gently carried us into friendships, quiet adventures, and a kind of strength that only stillness can teach. Letters from cousins became tiny treasures we waited weeks for. Trunk calls at the local post office once every fifteen days were our windows into the city world we'd left behind.

Life slowed to the rhythm of the hills.

Power cuts were frequent – sometimes lasting days, even weeks. But instead of panic, there was peace. We adapted. We'd finish meals by sunset, do our homework under flickering candlelight, and fall asleep to the soft hum of insects and the comfort of conversations that didn't compete with screens.

I still remember my mother quietly dropping Tulsi leaves into our clay water matka, her gentle way of blessing us with health and harmony.

And in that slower pace, we noticed more.

We climbed Jamun trees, bursting into giggles with purple-stained hands and shirts. We built treehouses on the banyan tree. We trudged through mucky monsoon lanes in thick rubber Duckback gumboots, and before stepping indoors, we'd wash our feet at the low stone sink just outside the house.

The red earth clung to us, as if the land itself didn't want to let us go.

The monsoons were like a magic show. When the rains arrived, they didn't tiptoe in – they poured down in sheets, turning the red soil into sticky clay and the hills into waterfalls. With the monsoon came our friends from Mahabaleshwar, migrating to Panchgani for the season like clockwork. The streets would come alive with the smell of roasted corn, hot chana wrapped in newspaper cones, and the sizzle of something always being fried nearby.

Back then, there were no fancy restaurants, no shiny cafes, and definitely no pizzerias with chalkboard menus. The food was simple and soulful. There was one legendary wada pav stall that fed half the town. If you were lucky, you'd get a hot aloo paratha from Akbarali's. *Unwalas* – the one-stop shop that sold everything from chocolates to sewing thread. That was our weekend outing – and truly, it was more than enough.

My brother, ever the city boy, spent vacations in Mumbai. But I stayed. I was in love, wildly and deeply, with this town.

Panchgani had its own quiet rhythm. With its winding, narrow lanes and whispering rains, it felt like the town breathed gently. During strawberry season, the fruit carts would pop up like magic, their baskets full of red, juicy berries. A soft bun pav and cream rolls from Lucky Bakery – still warm, wrapped in old newspaper – were a treat we never got tired of. The newspaper arrived a day late at the National Store, where the uncle behind the counter always knew which paper mattered to whom.

Life had a background score – the echoing azaan from the mosque, the Ganpati aarti with drums and bells, and the soft, steady toll of the church bell drifting through the valley on quiet mornings. Everything we needed was within a short walk: a small stationery shop for pencils and erasers, a tailor who always took a day longer than promised, and a grocer who gave you sweets with your change. Just one small lane was our entire market.

There was no rush, no race, no competition. Life was simple. We didn't need malls or megastores – the whole town ran on trust, time, and tiny daily routines.

This town didn't just grow on me – it grew into me

One summer, when I was seven, my mother handed me a slender sapling.

"This is your Gulmohar," she said, pointing to a small sapling no taller than me. "Water it every day." That moment became my ritual, my sacred pause between school and home. No matter how tired I was, I would rush back, still in uniform, fill up my tiny red bucket – the one that splashed more than it held – and walk with the solemn duty of a little gardener on a mission.

And I did. I watered that tree with the quiet reverence only children possess – the kind of belief that trees had hearts, that leaves whispered secrets, and that roots remembered kindness. Day after day, in sun and drizzle, I poured not just water, but wonder into that patch of soil.

As I grew, so did my Gulmohar – leaf by leaf, branch by branch, like a mirror to my own childhood. Its delicate green slowly turned into bold, reaching limbs. Birds began to visit. The wind began to sing in its branches. And then, one monsoon morning, something changed. I stepped out and saw that it had grown taller than me.

There I stood – a skinny, rain-soaked girl with muddy feet and wide eyes – staring up at this red-crowned giant I had helped raise. The clouds rolled above us, the raindrops tapped their approval on my shoulders, and for a fleeting moment, time paused.

It was a private triumph... quiet and powerful. As if, in my own small way, I had helped time do something beautiful. As if, through that tree, I had grown into something too.

Decades later, I took my children to meet that tree.

It still stands tall, proud, throwing wide shadows like open arms.

A silent witness to my childhood.

It's not just a tree. It's a part of me – a chapter that continues to breathe.

Eventually, the time came to leave. Like most children from small towns, I left for college, and then life happened. I moved to the city. The transition was slow and jarring – the noise, the pace, the distance – it took me years to adjust. *Time, like the tide, pulled me forward.* But it could never fully pull Panchgani out of me.

Every year, when I return to Panchgani, it stings a little more each time. The silence that once sang is now drowned in engines and selfies. What was once a forest is now a façade.

Over 500 bungalows, countless hotels, loud tourists demanding Wi-Fi and waffles in the land of wildflowers and stillness.

They come to the hills craving for the city.

But I wish – oh, I wish – they came for the right things.

For the whistling schoolboy's (bird) melodious tune during the rains.

For the crickets buzzing in concert as night falls. The misty fog during monsoons is like you are residing in a cloud.

For the fireflies glowing like fallen stars, tangled in the bushes. I still remember those tiny yellow blooms carpeting Tableland, as though the hills had laid out a floral bed to lull our childhood afternoons into magic.

I wish they'd sit still. Just once.

Close their eyes and truly listen.

Because if you do, the hills still speak.

—

I've made peace with the truth that change is inevitable.

That time flows, unasked and unstoppable.

But I've also learned: not all change is growth.

And not all noise is life.

So when the deadlines scream, when the horns blare, and the world feels a little too much –

I close my eyes.

And I'm there again.

Barefoot under my Gulmohar tree.

Red petals beneath me.

The breeze laced with memory.

A little girl, untamed and free,

listening for the echo of a church bell across the Sahyadri's.

Because time may move forward.

But it's tides...

...they always carry us back to where we truly belong.

~

34

A Trip Down Memory Lane

~ Bijal Pratik Shah

"Hurray!"

"Vacation begins!"

"Now it's play time!"

"No more studies!"

"Yaaaaayyy!"

Hearing the excited cheer of the children, Astha laughed and could not help but feel excited herself. The exams were over, and the summer break had just begun.

The kids were planning the activities they wanted to do over the holidays; some were travelling, some were joining a summer camp, some were just planning play dates. There was happiness and excitement all around, and the air was bustling with the holiday fever.

Astha's six-year-old son, Virat, was telling her all about his holiday plans, swimming every day, joining a sports camp, calling friends home, sleepovers, visiting parks and beaches, bowling, and video games at Funcity and Timezone in the malls, movie time, and so on.

Hearing his non-stop banter, a nostalgic smile played

on Astha's lips, and her mind drifted back to the childhood vacations they used to have.

That was so long ago. Seems like a lifetime. And they were so very different.

"Astha, Arjun, do not take too many toys. The bags are already full."

That was her mom telling her and her younger brother to decide what few toys they wanted to take to their maternal and paternal grandmothers' house, that is where they would be spending most of their holidays with their extended family. In those days, almost everyone went to their hometown to their grandparents' house during the summer vacation.

"Choo choo choo choo choo," A train whistled somewhere in the distance, and lo! She was at Bandra Station with her mom and Arjun, looking for their bogie. Her mom's voice still echoed in her ears, "Astha, *c'mon*, walk fast, we will miss our train."

Oh yes, her most favourite part of the holidays – the train journey. From the playful fights to who will be the first to get the window seat, making those scary noises when the train passes through the dark tunnels, waiting for the 'chai-wala uncle', savouring the packed yummy *'theplas'* with pickles, playing dumb charades and card games on the top berth, and running around the compartment – it was all so exciting. Meanwhile, the farms, forests, and villages whisked by in a blur of colour and life.

Finally, after what seemed to be an eternity (though it was just eight hours), the station Astha and Arjun had been eagerly waiting for arrived. The train slowed to a halt, and as soon as it stopped, they jumped down. And whoa, look who was there to welcome them... their entire gang of cousins. Ami, Snehal, Rashi, Anuj, Dhara, Devanshi, Madhvi, Chintan, Meera, Vismay, Rinku, and Anand, along with their uncle, all of whom were excitedly coming towards them.

It was a sight to behold. They all hugged each other. Everyone was talking at the same time, after all, they were meeting each other exactly a year after. They were all her paternal cousins, some first, some second, and some were third cousins, spread over different parts of the country – Mumbai, Surat, Vadodara, Kolkata, Bengaluru, Delhi.

In those days, there was no social media to keep us constantly connected or updated on each other's daily lives. Fortunately, everyone's vacations coincided, so we could all visit our hometown together.

The way to the grandmother's house was even more fun with everyone somehow fitting in one big six-seater auto rickshaw (called 'chhagda'). She could still visualize her grandparents waiting on the veranda, and the joy and love overflowing in their eyes on seeing them.

The house was a huge, three-storey bungalow – usually quiet, but now full of the sounds of running feet, children's laughter, mothers scolding their kids to be careful, the elders chit-chatting, and, of course, the tempting aroma of delicious dishes being cooked in the kitchen. It was their home – a place where one always felt loved and welcomed.

Astha remembered the long conversations they used to have under the starry nights on the terrace – catching up on each other's lives, discussions on any and every topic under the sun, and still whispering long into the night after all the elders were asleep. They all used to sleep on the terrace with mattresses lined up next to each other. Waking up late in the mornings was the undisputed norm, although their mothers tried hard to change that!

She could still imagine herself in that house, enjoying the long, lazy afternoons – swinging high and fast on one of the wooden swings, loud Bollywood music playing on the radio, singing her heart out while playing 'antakshari', watching back-to-back movies on TV, waiting for the 'kulfi-wala' uncle, playing cards, hopscotch and various board games like Ludo, Snakes & Ladders, Chess, Business, Cluedo, Pictionary – the list was long.

The smell and taste of all the delicious delicacies made by her grandmother and aunts were still fresh in her memory, as if it was only yesterday.

Evenings were filled with exploring the markets, visiting local sights, eating ice creams and 'golas' (ice slush) every night.

Their days and nights were a mix of laughing at silly jokes, teasing one another, arguing and quarrelling over trivial things, and making plans for the next time they would meet. Life felt complete – full of love, laughter, and happiness – with her dear ones around.

Memories overlapped in her mind, flooding her heart as she recalled the cherished times spent with her cousins, aunts, uncles, and grandparents.

She wished she could relive those moments – moments that had shaped her relationships and deepened her connection with her cousins, even the distant ones.

"Mom, are you even listening?"

"Where are you lost?"

"What happened, Mom?"

"Why are you crying and smiling at the same time?"

Virat's voice brought Astha back to the present. She looked lovingly at her only son, and thought how much this generation is missing out on the bonding with their extended families, especially those who are not in the same city.

Life has changed so much. With social media, you can be in touch with anyone, anywhere in the world – send a message on their special occasions, and keep up with each other's lives through Instagram and Facebook. But she could not help but wonder: Where is the physical presence, the emotional connection, in all of this?

Most of today's kids do not even know all their second cousins, forget about the third. Schools have vacations at different times; people plan holidays to visit and explore new places. Going to their hometowns is at the bottom of the list. Gadgets and social media have replaced people.

Of course, social media has its own advantages, but we must mindfully take a step back, slow down, and reintroduce our kids to meaningful family connections – especially the emotional bonds with extended family. This is increasingly important as family structures have shifted from large joint families to smaller nuclear units of just three or four members.

In today's fast-paced world, where everyone is caught up in their busy schedules, spending time with distant cousins and extended family can be challenging. However, even one small step in that direction can help bring our kids closer to one another. From there, social media can play its part in keeping those connections alive and thriving.

As it is rightly said that *'Change is the only thing which is Constant,'* we need to adapt to it, find a balance, and make the most of it so that we are still emotionally connected to our loved ones despite long distances separating us.

~

35

A Vacation, a Lost Phone & the Miracle of Midnight

~ Meghana Chandrachud

We picked the hottest month of the year to escape the city – and somehow, it turned into the craziest holiday of our lives. Malvan, a small coastal town in Maharashtra, near Goa, was our chosen destination. The plan: book a beach-facing villa far from Goa's bustle, feast on local seafood, and maybe attempt scuba diving

So off we went in our three cars to this beach-facing villa – three couples and four children. All of us are middle-aged couples, with ages ranging between 43 and 50 years. All of us had boys of similar ages – Arjun, Amit, and Inay were all between 15 and 18, and our little girl, the youngest, was just 5!

We spent one whole day travelling. The roads were smooth, the seafood spicy and fresh – better than anything in Mumbai – and the prices as light as the sea breeze.

We arrived in the evening. The villa was beautiful with a view of the sea from almost all the bedrooms and the living room. Nestled in a grove of palm and fruit trees, which are native to the region; with the birds, the wind and the waves creating their music together, it was such an idyllic location.

The day after we arrived, the boys did not want to get out

of the villa. It seems it was too hot and they wanted to just 'chill' in their room, which equates to "Leave us alone with our gadgets and we won't bother you for the rest of our time here!"

Well, but then we also really needed the break from them and our routine. So, we let them be. Fortunately, or unfortunately, the wi-fi was surprisingly good and our phones were able to pick it up in all parts of the property. In the absence of a strong mobile network, we would still be connected. I am not that much of a phone person. But I like to stream music, so it was a blessing.

The view was scenic, and though the place was hot, the summer coolers and beers were flowing in the hot summer afternoon. There was a caretaker and a cook in the villa, so the rest of us decided to stay in as well after our long journey the day prior and enjoy the day in our luxurious villa.

The little one was happy to colour in her book and roam in the now familiar premises and play with the caretaker's daughter... all I had to do was make sure she ate something, and she was sorted!

After a lazy afternoon, Anjali and I decided it would be a good idea to take a walk along the beach. The men decided to have their tea indoors. Priya, our other friend, was still taking a nap, so we decided to let her relax.

By then, the day was tilting gently towards evening, the sun's harshness giving way to a softer gold. The tide had begun its slow retreat – nature's own clock marking the hours in a language older than any watch.

As luck would have it, the sun was less strong now that it was 5 p.m. To our joy and surprise, the boys decided to come to the beach with us – they wanted to get into the water. It seemed like such a good idea to us. They had come out of their room voluntarily without any prodding on our part. The only other time in the day we saw them was when they got hungry and wanted lunch or a snack (which they asked the caretaker to give them), so it was a welcome change for us.

A small road separated the villa from the beach. The sea was not very calm, but it was not turbulent either. A gentle breeze was blowing, and the beautiful coconut trees were swaying. The calming sound of the waves felt almost like breathing – a rhythm that reminded me that time moves differently by the sea.

One of the boys, Arjun, Priya's son, got a plastic chair from the house. He said that he did not feel like going into the water immediately. He just wanted to sit and feel the waves on his feet.

Anjali and I were strolling along the beach. It was such a tranquil scene. One that we had longed for in the company of friends who were so dear to us. We connect in the city. But when you travel together and live together, the bond is always different, and that's what we wanted to enjoy.

We had gone a long way off along the beach. We turned back to go towards the boys. Arjun was sitting in the chair with a phone in his hand, filming the other two boys who were splashing around in the water and joking and generally having a good time like boys of that age do.

As we got closer, Arjun said he wanted to go into the water. Anjali insisted that he give her his phone and earbuds that he was wearing. Promptly, he handed over his earbuds and said he wanted to go in the water to film his friends. He said that his phone was waterproof. Before she could refute it, he put the phone in the pocket of his shorts, and before we knew what was happening, he jumped straight into the water.

In the next two seconds, he realised his phone had fallen out of his pocket and into the sea. The tide, which had seemed gentle a moment ago, now felt like a thief, gobbling up a precious thing in seconds. What followed was a completely helpless feeling and a frantic search for the phone because the immediate reaction would have to be just that! Later, when we could not find the phone in the muddy water, all hell broke loose. The parents were in the house, and an expensive iPhone Pro of the latest configuration had been swallowed by the sea!

We called all the others. Even my little daughter came to the beach, and all of us searched in the sea for one long hour along an unfamiliar Malvan coastline. The tide was picking up, and soon, it would be too dark to get into the water. We decided to stop our search and head back to our villa. It felt like we had lost a battle. The day's light had slipped away while we searched – proof that both time and tide wait for no one.

So much disappointment on Day 1 of our trip! There were raised voices and a lot of unpleasant things said to Arjun like "We should never have gotten you this new phone on your birthday," and "You have no value for the things you get," etc. Our peaceful summer break was not going according to plan. All he said was, "My phone is waterproof and nothing will happen to it."

But how was it going to come out of the sea?!

After much discussion, we decided it would be futile to look for the phone now.

However, we still enquired when it would be low tide. There was an off-chance that we would still be able to get it back. We learned from the locals that low tide was after 11:30 p.m. - late in the night. We were disappointed. How in heaven's name were we to search for a small three-inch by six-inch object in this enormous ocean in the middle of the night?

We were losing hope. The mood was sombre and the conversations minimal. The loss of an expensive phone was a big blow to the boy and his parents, and also to us onlookers who couldn't believe the incredulous unfolding of events!

Nevertheless, we decided to give it one last shot.

The little one was asleep, and I made sure she was tucked in comfortably.

After 11:30 p.m., the rest of us decided to try one last time, five hours after we had lost the phone. Hoping against hope that the sea would spit out the phone just like all the other rubbish that humans throw into it. We set off, equipped with resolve and two torches borrowed from the house, and all our phones. A brief murmur about how the phone is gone forever was firmly silenced by me prodding the rest not to give up hope.

The search began – we had only an approximate location, a completely muddy sea, and a dark night to give us company. The beach was deserted and dark. Not a single streetlight was in proximity. We switched on the borrowed torches and the torches on our phones. It felt almost timeless – a scene that could have belonged to another century, a group of people scanning the shore for something precious the ocean had claimed.

After forty minutes of searching, there was still no sign of the phone, and we were fast losing faith. I felt like we were combing the sea in knee-deep water on a black night. Circumstance and fate both seemed to be on the opposite side. We were fighting a losing battle against hope.

Priya, Arjun's mother, was chanting continuously. She does Tibetan chanting. She called me and said, "What shall we do now?" I said, "Why don't you try to ring the phone?" She said she had tried, and it was switched off. I told her to try again. Again, she got the same response. Then I told her to call on WhatsApp. She tried. It said "Calling" and not "Ringing." She was beginning to think it was futile. I was praying and giving her company, she was chanting, and the rest were searching. Everyone was drained mentally, emotionally, and physically. This event was taxing our brains and our bodies, and there was nothing any of us could do about it.

The atmosphere was tense. I told her to keep trying. She said she had tried three times and things were the same. Finally, I said, "Give me the phone. Let me try this time."

I decided to try another WhatsApp call on his phone, all the time praying the wi-fi would catch. The night was quiet. There was no other disturbance. I was sure it would catch. The distance was not too great, and the wi-fi was strong. I pressed the dialer, saying "Come on, come on," under my breath.

Arjun's father, Kishore, was in knee-deep water and right next to him in the dark sea, something flashed... it was a light coming from the water. He bent down and touched it. Then he picked it up. Sure enough, he had found the phone!

That moment was pure joy... the once silent beach became a frenzy of animated people, shouting excitedly! It was unbelievable!

Hours earlier, the tide had taken it away. Now, at its lowest, it had given it back. Time and tide had played their game, and for once, we'd been on the winning side.

We had found the phone with almost no hope, no equipment, and when the chances were less than one in a million! Just goes to show that belief, luck, and faith are all real and they can all work miracles!

I can still hear Arjun's voice after the whole adventure, or misadventure.

Ironically, he was saying, "I told you. My phone is waterproof, and nothing will happen to it."

Anyway, the phone still works, and the rest of the holiday was peaceful and uneventful.

But for me, that night was a reminder that the passage of hours, the rise and fall of the tide, and the patience to wait for the right moment can turn a near-loss into a story we'll carry for a lifetime.

~

36

A Promise Kept - Across Time

~ Anannya Sane

Wai was the kind of village where everyone knew everyone. At its heart stood a giant banyan tree – the kind with roots so thick that we used to pretend they were dragon tails. My grandmother said the tree was over two hundred years old and that as a kid, she had heard tales about the tree glowing silver at night. I never really believed her, not until Sehar came into my life.

I still remember the first time I met Sehar. We had just moved into our new house. I was around three years old, sitting on my veranda, eating a piece of jaggery, when this little girl came hopping from the neighbouring house. Her fists were full of crushed marigolds from her garden, with the petals sticking to her sweaty palms. "For you," she said, with a big smile on her face. Instantly, I reciprocated her gesture by giving her my half-eaten jaggery piece. That's how it began.

Sehar was a petite girl of cheerful demeanour, sunshine and stories all wrapped in one. The dusky glow of her skin wasn't just a trait; it was a visible aura. Even as a young girl, her mind was a whirlpool of curiosity, making her the undisputed star of the village. You could often find her with a book, her fingers tracing the words as if she could pull the stories into her very being, and when she wasn't reading, she was spinning her own tales; her voice could transform a mundane afternoon into an epic adventure. A perpetual twinkle always danced in her eyes, as if it held a secret of a thousand faraway lands she visited only in her mind.

Skies always fascinated Sehar; she was always looking up, trying to find something interesting there. Even while walking, she would be staring at the sky, tripping over stones, but never caring. "Look, Tara!" she'd say, pointing at some bird I couldn't even see. But it was the night sky that really captured her.

By the time we were ten, we were inseparable – Sehar with her wild curls that never stayed in her braid, I with my two tight plaits. Every morning we'd walk to school holding hands, our tiffin boxes clinking in our bags. The village aunties would smile and say we were like Radha and Krishna.

But our real adventures happened after school. We would run straight to the old banyan tree, where Sehar would pull out whatever book she could borrow from the school library. She read as if she were starving, gulping down stories about princesses, space travel, and girls like Malala, who changed the world. I liked listening more than reading. There was something magical about how Sehar's voice changed when she read, like she wasn't just telling a story but living it.

Every night after dinner, she would sneak into our veranda for a bit, and we would sit with our necks craned backward. Sehar would explain the constellations in that excited voice she used for her favourite stories. "See those seven stars? That's Saptarishi!" Her finger would trace invisible lines between stars while I squinted, trying to see what she saw. "And that one is the Dhruv tara, it has a fixed spot". Our session would end abruptly when Sehar's mother would call out for her.

When we got older, Sehar started borrowing astronomy books from our school's tiny library. She would read them to me under the banyan tree, "One day I'm going to be up there," she'd say, pointing to the sky. "Just like Kalpana Chawla."

I remember the exact moment she discovered Kalpana's story. We were fifteen, at the yearly book fair in town. Sehar found this dog-eared biography with Kalpana's smiling face on the cover. She clutched it to her chest like it was made of gold. "She's from Haryana, Tara! Just a normal girl who reached space!"

That book never left her side. She read it under our tree, at lunch, even walking home from school. At night, we'd sit on our veranda as usual, but now instead of just pointing out constellations, she'd tell me about zero gravity and space stations. "Imagine seeing our whole village from up there," she'd whisper, eyes shining with starlight. "Just a tiny dot between the hills."

When we turned seventeen, Sehar found a tattered copy of a magazine at the yearly book fair, which featured an interview with Sunita Williams, sharing about her first space travel and her training for the next. For weeks, we sat under our tree while she read it aloud. I remember how her fingers trembled while turning the pages. It appeared as if Sehar had almost transcended to space thereafter.

Things got even more exciting when Tara's father got a smartphone. We spent whole afternoons huddled around that tiny screen, watching videos of Kalpana Chawla and Sunita Williams floating in the International Space Station. Sehar would press her nose to the screen, as if she wanted to climb through it. "That's going to be me one day!" she'd say with absolute certainty.

One day, Sehar came running up to me, her eyes shining and face all lit up. "Tara, I have a brilliant idea, we should write down our dreams, like promises. Once we turn twenty-five, we can open them and see how much of it has come true."

That's how we ended up burying a rusty biscuit tin under the tree. Inside were two notes wrapped in brown paper from the grocery store, with our respective names written on them – 'Sehar' and 'Tara'. We pinky promised we would dig it up when we turned twenty-five.

Then one Tuesday, all hell broke loose. Sehar had been fine that morning, laughing as she tried to climb the banyan tree's highest root, telling me about a new star she had spotted. That evening, we were supposed to watch a meteor shower from our veranda. But instead, her mother came running to our house, face white as chalk. "Help! Sehar has just collapsed and is not responding at all. We need to take her to the hospital right now."

At the hospital, the doctor kept using words like "sudden" and "unexpected". Almost half the village was outside, trying to figure out what had happened and be of help at the same time. The chaos was deafening to me. I stood there with a bated breath, holding Sehar's hand, waiting for her to wake up and tell me about tonight's meteor shower. But her fingers grew cold and the nurses started giving me those pitying looks. My mother softly cushioned my head with her hands and pulled me towards her. "She is gone, beta." That's when I screamed – really screamed – until my throat hurt, and my father had to carry me home.

My whole world had come crashing down. For months, I barely left my bed. The banyan tree stood empty, our swing motionless. Finally, my father decided we were moving to Nashik. "A fresh start," he called it. I didn't care. I just packed my clothes and the notebook where I had written down all of Sehar's favourite stories.

Nashik was loud and bright and full of people who didn't know me as "Sehar's other half." Slowly, piece by piece, I put myself back together. I studied like my life depended on it – because in a way, it did.

Years passed. I got into medical college and became "Dr. Tara" – my dream had finally come true! But the joy of accomplishment was missing; I dearly craved Sehar's presence.

Then, last month, an invitation came. My old school in Wai wanted to honour me as their first student to become a doctor. I hadn't been back since that terrible day, but something pulled me there.

The village now looked smaller. That evening, after the function got over, my heart was flooded with feelings that I cannot put into words. As I walked towards Sehar's house, I spotted the banyan tree from a distance. Thousands of happy memories suddenly flashed through my mind, and I decided to walk up to the tree and sit underneath, in memory of my dearest Sehar. The root under my fingers felt familiar, as if I was holding hands with an old friend. Then suddenly I remembered – the tin. We were supposed to open it at twenty-five.

My hands shook as I dug near the biggest root. And there it was – rusted, but still whole. Inside, Sehar's note was faded but clear:

"I want to fly up there, into that endless sky where all the stars live. Not just see them from down here like tiny dots, but go right next to them, close enough to touch their light. I want to float between them, weightless, just like Kalpana Chawla and Sunita Williams. I want to take pictures of every star I meet – the big ones that burn blue, the small ones that flicker gold, and save them all to show Tara. And someday... I'll find the most beautiful star of all. One that glows extra bright, maybe in a constellation shaped like a banyan tree, and shall name it 'Sehar-Tara'. Then, we too shall have our own place in the universe forever."

As I read, a warm breeze circled me, though the air had been still. Then, I left one of the roots had moved. Just slightly, like it was brushing away my tears.

The tin creaked open by itself. Inside was a new note, which read :

"Couldn't be there to open this with you. Look in the hollow – left you one last story."

My heart pounded as I reached into the tree's hollow. There was a book with blank pages. But when I opened it, words appeared in Sehar's messy handwriting – our story. The day we met. The time we got caught in the rain. Our last afternoon together.

As I turned the last page, something glittering rose from the paper. It swirled up into the darkening sky, forming a new constellation. And there, between the stars, was a bright new star – shining at me like it knew a secret. I knew in that instant, this was our 'Sehar-Tara'!

I laughed through my tears. Some promises get kept in ways we never expect. There she was, in her favourite space amidst the stars, telling me that she had finally made it!

This year, I built an open library under the tree. At night, village kids read there by lantern light. Sometimes, when the wind turns the pages, I like to think it's Sehar, still telling her stories.

And if you look up on clear nights? You'll see a bright star – 'Sehar-tara' twinkle, reminding us that some special bonds can sail even through the tide of time.

~

37

To Trust Again

~ Shreya Khosla

I looked at the tall, thin girl standing before me. She appeared rather frail – she'd recently recovered from an illness, she'd told me. A glint of hope shone in her eyes as she requested my books, having missed several months of tenth grade, but scepticism loomed across her delicate features, anticipating my refusal to help.

I shook my head as I replied, pursing my lips, "I'm sorry, Nidhi, I cannot lend you my books. I need to study." I turned away and headed towards home.

As I lay in bed that night, pangs of guilt burdened my conscience and prevented me from sleeping. How could I have denied helping Nidhi, simply because of my experience five years earlier? As I wandered down memory lane, my mind began flashing unforgettable images from a time when I'd been so naïve, full of love and longing to help others.

It had started with a middle-aged, pleasant lady visiting our house and speaking to my mother in private. After she'd left, my mother briefed me about a girl named Vidhi, who was in my class. She'd suffered a personal loss that had deeply disturbed her, leaving her so distraught that she'd missed several months of school. Vidhi was frightened and nervous about returning to school after such a lengthy absence. My role was to help her settle back in, and as part of that, I needed to befriend her and assist with her studies.

I was absolutely thrilled by the idea! I adored helping others, and in this particular case, I wouldn't only be helping someone – I'd also be making a new friend. I could spend time with Vidhi, play with her, study with her. The prospect of all the activities we could enjoy together truly excited me.

And so the journey began. We met at school the following day, and her mother – the same lady who'd visited our house – introduced us formally.

"Shreya, this is my daughter Vidhi," she said warmly. "I do hope you two will become good friends."

"Hello, Vidhi," I said with a bright smile. "I'm looking forward to getting to know you."

The teacher made us benchmates. Initially, Vidhi hardly spoke, and my mother had cautioned me beforehand.

"Don't ask her personal questions, Shreya," she'd warned. "It could hurt her feelings."

So I tried discussing her favourite books, the teachers, the school, her preferred subjects, and her favourite television programmes. Gradually, by the end of one week, we'd hit it off splendidly. We began spending considerable time together at school – exchanging notes, explaining topics to each other, and even sharing our snacks and lunch during breaks.

There were occasions when her mother visited during lunch break, carrying a basket brimming with food. In those days, the school still allowed mothers to bring lunch for their children – oh, what wonderfully carefree times! Since we'd become inseparable, I'd carry my lunchbox and sit with her and her mother.

"Shreya, dear, I've brought your favourite sandwiches today," her mother would say kindly.

Sometimes she brought pizzas with extra pieces for me, and I'd happily give my lunchbox a miss on those delightful occasions.

Whilst Vidhi and I spent nearly all our school time together, we'd also begun having weekend playdates. Sometimes she'd visit my house, and occasionally I'd go to hers. She lived in a magnificent bungalow, and it was tremendous fun running about and playing games there, so gradually it became our regular hangout spot. Her mother grew quite fond of me and began preparing my favourite dishes. It felt as though I had another family alongside my own loving one.

That's when I allowed myself to imagine a future where Vidhi and I would remain friends forever, even as adults – chatting with each other, discussing everything, rather like the way my mother and grandmother gossiped with their friends and relatives.

But as they say, all good things must come to an end. I'd allowed my heart to trust completely. She'd become an integral part of my life, but somehow, gradually, I lost my place in hers. Several girls at school, jealous of our friendship, had been working to create misunderstandings between us.

It was the beginning of seventh grade. We hadn't spent much time together during the summer holidays because both families had travel plans. As the new term commenced, I was excited to see her and had planned how we might spend our days together.

I entered school, bubbling with anticipation for the day ahead. There she stood – confident and cheerful – chatting with other girls. I remembered how she'd been a year earlier: nervous, unable to hold conversations with anyone. I was delighted to witness her transformation.

I rushed over and called out, "Hi, Vidhi!"

But she glanced at me and turned away. She didn't sit beside me and didn't speak to me the entire day. I was utterly baffled by this behaviour, constantly wondering whether I'd done something wrong to hurt her, whether I'd said something inappropriate. What had I done to make her so cold towards me?

I didn't understand what had happened, so I returned home and confided in my mother.

"Darling, you should confront her," she advised. "Speak your heart out to her. Perhaps there's been a misunderstanding."

That's precisely what I decided to do. The next day, as she chatted with other friends, I approached again.

"Hi, Vidhi!" I called cheerfully.

As she turned away, I persisted, "Vidhi, could we speak privately?"

She ignored me, so I gently took her arm. "What's happened, Vidhi? Why won't you talk to me? Why are you avoiding me?"

She looked at me and, in front of the other girls, declared coldly, "Shreya, you've used me for your own advantage. You prevented me from making any new friends besides yourself, and then you constantly told my mother to cook this and that for you. You're always at my house – I don't like it."

I was absolutely stunned. I had taken advantage of her? Was she being serious? Despite my shock, for the sake of our beautiful friendship, I replied, "Listen, it's nothing like that. Let's talk and sort this out."

"I don't want to speak to you ever again," she said firmly. "I don't want to be your friend anymore."

With that, she walked away.

I was completely dumbfounded and returned to my desk. I remember zoning out for the remainder of that day. I went home and wept bitterly. All her accusations were utterly false – I'd never invited myself to her house; it had always been her or her mother who'd called me over. I'd never asked her mother to cook for me; she'd done so out of love. I'd lent her my books, taught her everything she'd missed – yet despite all this, I had apparently taken advantage of her! It was completely incredulous.

The following days were tremendously difficult because I was hurt by her accusations and even more wounded by her behaviour towards me. However, I couldn't miss school because of her.

That's when I toughened myself and built a boundary around my heart – no one would be permitted to enter it anymore. No more helping anyone, no more befriending them. That's how I spent the next four years.

Then suddenly, today, Nidhi – a girl from my class who'd missed a considerable period of school due to illness – approached me, requesting my books. The moment she asked for help, the boundary I'd created tightened, refusing to allow me to fall into that trap and suffer hurt again. Because of this protective wall, I'd made an excuse and walked away from the situation.

But I suppose one's nature doesn't truly change. The very fact that I'd refused to help someone who genuinely needed assistance prevented me from sleeping. I tossed and turned whilst the good and evil sides of me debated fiercely:

The good me whispered, "You should have helped her."

The evil me rejected this firmly: "Help and then get hurt again? Absolutely not. All these girls are the same – they'll seek help, and once they have what they need, they'll have nothing to do with you. There's no need to help."

The good me continued, "Not all fingers on your hand are identical – not everyone possesses the same nature. Just because one person has hurt you doesn't mean you shouldn't help anyone else throughout your life! It's your nature to help others – don't resist it!"

The debate continued until both sides of me reached a consensus, and I managed to catch a couple of hours' sleep. In the morning, as I prepared for school, I'd made up my mind. Time had taught me that one couldn't trust blindly or too hastily, but that didn't mean one couldn't help others at all! If doing something brought me joy, I would do it – but I'd tread those murky waters carefully.

As I arrived at school, I approached Nidhi and asked, "Hello! Did you manage to get the books from someone else?"

"No," she replied, disappointment flickering across her face.

"Right then. You may borrow my books – these cover all subjects except mathematics," I said, handing her a large package of notebooks. "I'm currently studying maths, so could you complete these within the next week or ten days? I'll give you the mathematics books afterwards."

She gratefully accepted the books and gave me a thankful smile. I smiled back, and it made my heart feel lighter and happier. As I turned to head to class, she called out nervously, "Could you give me your number? Also, would you like to spend time together tomorrow after school? We could study for a while and then watch some television together?"

"Tread carefully," my inner voice cautioned, reminding me to protect myself from being hurt again, "but don't stop trusting," it added gently.

That's when I smiled and nodded warmly, "Certainly, let's spend time together."

~

38

The Search of Silver Stars

~ Nidhi Shah

Watching the Stars

He called them silver stars – small, shining hopes hidden in ordinary nights.

When Anaya was five, her father lifted her onto his shoulders and walked to the field behind their house. Beneath constellations, he'd point upward, telling her stars weren't just balls of fire.

"They're promises," he said. "The sky keeps them until we're ready."

She didn't understand then. She only knew that his voice was calm, the world safe with his hand on her back. Each night, as they searched the sky, he let her name a new silver star – after dreams, questions, or fears. He never corrected her when she renamed the same one, simply nodding as if each name made it shine brighter.

Rain, Mango, and Papa's Laugh

At seven, Anaya brimmed with curiosity and energy. She collected pebbles, drew suns with squiggly rays, and jumped into puddles – even when Mama warned, "You'll catch a cold and turn into a frog!"

Papa, Mr. Girish, was busy but his quiet laugh made her

feel safe. His Sunday breakfasts were famous: toast, mango pickle (spicy enough to make her giggle and cry), and tea with far too much sugar – "Sweet enough for a princess," he said.

One morning, she asked, "Papa, why don't clouds fall down?"

He scratched his head. "Because they're lazy, like someone I know who never makes her bed."

"Hey! I do make my bed... sometimes."

"Yes – usually when a spider's hiding in there."

School Struggles and Secret Tears

School wasn't as fun as puddles. Anaya was slow in math, and when she read aloud, her voice was so soft it sounded like a mouse sneezing. Once, when the answer was eleven, she confidently said, "Seven."

Classmates chuckled. "Nice try, Anaya. You're confusing math with magic."

That night she came home quiet. Papa noticed.

"Bad day?"

She shrugged. "I'm not smart."

Papa opened his dusty star book. "Do you know how long it takes the sun to rise?"

"No."

"Exactly. But it still rises. Even when it's lazy."

"Maybe I'm just a lazy star."

"Then you're the brightest lazy star I know."

The Great Water Spill

During art class, Anaya was excited to paint her cat. She filled her water cup but – SPLASH! – spilled it all over Riya's drawing.

"You ruined my masterpiece!" Riya cried.

The teacher looked faint. Anaya froze – then tried hiding under the table.

Later Papa joked, "If hiding were an Olympic sport, you'd be a gold medalist."

After school, she was too scared to face anyone. Papa came with a broken pencil. He snapped it and taped it back together.

"See? Even broken things can still write stories – and get out of trouble!"

She laughed for the first time that day.

The Muddy Race

Anaya signed up for the 200-metre race. She wasn't the fastest – more a snail in sneakers – but she wanted to try.

On race day, rain poured, turning the track into mud soup.

At the start she ran carefully – until she slipped, SPLAT, into a puddle.

The crowd gasped, then laughed. Soaked and muddy, she felt like a ruined chocolate cake.

Papa, on the sidelines, put his hand on his heart and winked.

She stood, smiled, and finished like a muddy superhero.

Later Papa said, "Who needs a trophy when you've got mud on your knees and a smile on your face?"

Night Chats and Magic Journals

After stories and brushing teeth, Anaya and Papa had a secret ritual – nightly chats with God.

She kept a “magic journal” filled with scribbles, drawings, and hopes.

“Ready for our nightly chat?” Papa asked in his “news anchor” voice.

“Yes, Mr. Anchor!” she giggled.

Their prayers were simple, honest words.

“Dear God,” Anaya said once, “thank you for the sun that hides so I can wear rain boots.”

Papa added, “And thank you for making my daughter brave enough to fall in the mud and get up again.”

In her journal she wrote: “I spilled water on Riya’s drawing. Oops. But Papa said even broken pencils can still write stories. Tomorrow I’ll try to be careful. Also, I want to be brave like Papa when he tells jokes.”

“Every day is a new story,” Papa smiled, “and you’re the writer.”

As he tucked her in, he whispered, “Remember, little star, when you talk to God, He listens. And when you write, you remember you’re brave.”

“Goodnight, Papa. Goodnight, God.”

Mama: The Secret Superhero

While Papa was full of jokes and wisdom, Mama was the strong engine keeping the family train on track. Always on her toes – cooking, working, paying bills, fixing buttons, remembering everyone’s passwords – she was a superhero with a calendar instead of a cape.

Once, Anaya had a science project due the next day: a working dam. “Don’t worry,” Mama said, rolling up her sleeves.

By morning she had built a model village with dam, river, bridge and boats – from cardboard, straws, and a spoon.

Papa saw it and said, "Should I just retire now?"

"I think Mama loves you more than me," Anaya whispered.

Papa whispered back, "Maybe. But don't tell her I love you both more than she knows."

Mama smiled into her tea. Even when she scolded, her eyes shone with pride. Every time Anaya fell, Mama was there – steady, supportive, always with a towel.

Brave Like Me

It began small – whispers in the hallway, snickers in the lunch line.

"Why the same ponytail?"

"Your voice is squeaky."

"Did you mess up again?"

They were just kids, but words hurt.

One afternoon Anaya tripped on her shoelace, falling on her books. A few laughed cruelly. "Nice move, Anaya. Joining the circus?"

She blinked back tears, heart like a deflated balloon.

That night at dinner she barely touched pizza.

"You okay, pumpkin?" Papa asked.

She shrugged. "It's nothing."

Mama's look pierced through. She hugged her. "Tell us. Even the hard things."

The tears came. She told them about whispers, laughs, and not belonging.

Papa was quiet, then said, "Even the moon has craters. Yet people stare in wonder."

Mama added, "When someone tries to make you small, it's their own smallness showing. You carry silver stars."

They didn't promise the world would change, only to stand beside her while she did.

The Kind Comeback

"Don't be silly," Arjun said when Meera flushed after tripping on a rock.

"Clumsy? You saved the basket from falling – that's skill!" His teasing warmth dissolved her embarrassment into laughter.

Arjun's knack for turning mishaps into humour amazed her. Where others might have rolled their eyes, he infused lightness.

Meera smiled long after, heart lighter – not for the stumble, but for being seen with kindness.

The Teacher Who Believed in Me

School wasn't always easy, but one special person changed everything – her teacher, Ms. Gandhi. She wasn't just a teacher; she had the magic of seeing what others missed.

One day, after class, Ms.Gandhi asked, "Do you know how wonderfully weird your imagination is?"

Anaya blinked. No one had called her imagination "wonderful" before.

Ms. Gandhi gave her creative writing prompts and encouraged her to join the school's storytelling contest. When Anaya hesitated, she said, "You're not here to be perfect. You're here to be real."

With Ms. Gandhi's help, Anaya began shining – writing poems, solving math problems, and even volunteering for group projects.

When exam results came, Anaya had scored brilliantly.

"You did this," Ms. Gandhi said, "because you believed. And because someone believed in you too."

The Catch-Me Game

Anaya often played with a group of girls at recess – giggling, twirling, running in circles. From the outside, it looked like fun.

But inside, something didn't feel right.

They always played the same game.

"Let's play catch!" said Meenal, the leader.

"Yeah," added Gia. "Anaya, you always have to catch us!"

"Again?" Anaya asked, her smile fading.

"Of course," Meenal tossed her hair. "You're the fastest!"

But Anaya wasn't the fastest. She knew that wasn't why they wanted her chasing them. She would run and run while they squealed, whispered, and darted away. Every time she got close: "Too slow!"

It wasn't fun anymore.

One day she sat down, too tired to play.

"Ugh, you're no fun," Meenal rolled her eyes.

That evening, Anaya came home quiet. She sat by the window, watching raindrops race down the glass, her "magic journal" open but empty.

Papa found her there.

"Bad day?" he asked.

Anaya nodded. "I don't think they really like me. They just like running away."

Papa pulled out two socks – one with dots, one with stripes.

"Dotty Sock says, 'Let's play a game!' Stripey Sock says, 'Only if it's fair.' Dotty says, 'You always chase us.' Stripey replies, 'But I want to laugh with you, not just run after you.'"

Anaya smiled faintly. "That's a weird sock story."

Papa winked. "Sometimes weird stories hold big truths."

Finding Her Voice

The next day at recess, the game began again.

"Anaya, you're it!" Meenal shouted.

But Anaya didn't move. She took a deep breath.

"I don't want to play if I'm always chasing. That's not fun for me."

The girls stared. Gia whispered, "She's being moody again."

But Anaya stood tall. "Friends take turns. Friends don't make one person feel left out."

She walked away, unsure if it was right – but feeling something powerful in her chest: pride.

Later, a quiet girl named Saanya came to her by the swings.

"I saw what you said," she murmured. "Can I play with you?"

Anaya smiled. "Sure. But no chasing today – just flying high."

They pushed each other on the swings, laughing until the bell rang.

That night, Anaya wrote: *"Today I said no. Not because I was angry. But because I mattered too. It felt strange... but strong."*

Papa kissed her forehead. "You were brave."

"Brave like Stripey Sock," she whispered.

"Exactly," he laughed.

Later, she noticed a boy, Kabir, looking downcast. She sat beside him.

"Don't condemn yourself," she said softly. "I used to be scared too. But now I have a magic journal, a smart Papa, and a Mama who says I carry silver stars."

"I don't have stars," Kabir whispered.

"You do," Anaya said. "You just haven't found them yet."

That night she added: *"Today I helped someone else find his voice. I think courage grows when you pass it on, like a warm sandwich."*

A Hero for Someone Else

A week later, Anaya saw a little boy named Kabir being cornered near the swings.

"Crybaby Kabir!" someone shouted. He had tears in his eyes.

Anaya felt something rise inside her – not fear, but fire.

She stepped forward, put a hand on Kabir's shoulder, and said firmly, "Hey. That's not okay. Everyone deserves kindness."

The bullies shuffled away, surprised.

Growing Up With Laughter

As Anaya grew, she learned that life had serious moments – but also lots of silly, messy, and funny ones.

Like when she wore two different shoes to school and didn't notice until lunchtime.

Or, when Papa tried yoga with her and fell asleep during "downward dog."

Through all the ups and downs, laughter was their secret glue.

The Graduation Speech

Years later, Anaya stood at her graduation stage, ready to speak.

"I learned a lot from school," she said, "but the best lessons came from home. From a Papa who taught me how to laugh through mistakes, a Mama who built dams out of cardboard and dreams out of discipline, and a teacher who saw my spark."

The audience applauded.

Papa sat in the back, holding Mama's hand. He leaned in and whispered, "Still love you both more than the moon."

Mama smiled. "I heard that."

Years passed. The stars remained, but her father began to fade – first in memory, then in breath.

Anaya grew older. She stopped looking up.

But grief has a strange way of turning our gaze skyward again. One night, alone and unsure in a city far from home, she stepped outside and lifted her eyes. And there they were – those silver stars – quiet, patient, waiting. One of them shimmered with a flicker she recognized. She didn't know its name anymore, but she knew what it meant.

Her father had taught her how to find the light. Not just in the sky, but in herself.

And so, she searched – not for answers, but for the echoes of his voice in the quiet. For the constellations they named. For the stars that were really promises.

For the love that had never once stopped shining.

She wrote in her diary that day:

Life is full of muddy puddles, spilled water, and silly mistakes.

But with a little laughter, a lot of love, and someone standing quietly beside you –

you can do anything.

Thank you, Papa!

Thank you, God!

~ Excerpts from Pujya Gurudevshri's videos from SRMD website Be your best friend first.!

~

39

Fossils Raising Robots

~ Rita Choudhari

"You'll understand when you become a mom."

My mother used to say this with theatrical sighs and dramatic pauses, usually when I was arguing with her, ignoring her advice, or just being my teenage self, and acting like she knew nothing and I knew it all.

At the time, I'd roll my eyes so hard I could see my brain. "No way will I become that kind of mom," I told myself.

And yet - here I am!

Every time my daughter Annie disagrees with me or hits me with Gen Z wisdom, I hear my mother's voice echo in my head... followed by a gentle thud of guilt. It's like karma, but in high definition.

From the moment Annie was born, I've been on this rollercoaster of motherhood, watching her transform from a cuddly little bundle into a sharp-tongued, screen-glued high-schooler. Now, whenever she sighs at me like I'm the problem, I hear my mom's voice echoing in my head, giggling somewhere in the background, whispering, "Told you so."

That sigh, that subtle teenage eye-roll of a moment, was my official entry into the "you won't understand" zone.

I wasn't the cool, clued-in mom anymore. I'd been gently

promoted to "outdated but still trying." No matter how tech-savvy or open-minded we think we are, every mother eventually stumbles into that moment - the one where the generation gap doesn't just show up, it stares you in the face. And when it does, it's not just a gap – it's a canyon – Wi-Fi enabled, emoji-powered, full of phrases we don't fully understand.

Somewhere between bedtime lullabies and board exam stress, I genuinely believed I'd cracked the code of modern parenting. An educated, tech-savvy, open-minded mom – surely that would keep me forever relevant in my child's world.

To keep up, I even enrolled in a phonics course – yes, seriously, because I was determined to teach her the right way to pronounce everything. Fast forward a few years, and guess who's correcting me now? Every other sentence in our discussion comes with a grammar update, a pronunciation adjustment, and a side-eye.

There was a time, not too long ago, when parenting felt structured and predictable, at least somewhat. Annie was in primary school then – a soft-spoken, obedient child who listened to my advice like it was gospel. If I said, "This is how it's pronounced," she nodded with wide-eyed trust and never argued. Those were the golden days, when kids believed everything their parents said... mainly because they didn't know any better.

Back then, school meant getting up on time, wearing neatly ironed uniforms, eating a proper breakfast, and heading out with a water bottle and a bag bigger than the child. Worksheets were coming home, school circulars pinned to the fridge, weekends filled with art projects, extra classes, and sports activities.

And just when I thought I had this whole "modern mom" thing under control, came COVID – not just a wave, but a full-blown tsunami – dragging our sweet, innocent children into a world of screens, slang, and school-from-bed.

Sometimes I still wonder what that pandemic was really about. Was it nature's glitch? A manmade mess? Or maybe... just maybe... It was God's way of reminding us about karma in the form of a virus.

Whatever it was, it changed everything. Especially our children.

And so began the era of digital childhood. Now, Annie was a high school student, a soft-spoken, well-mannered girl who'd raise her hand and say "Excuse me, Ma'am," now attended math class lying in bed, half-covered with a blanket, hair in a bun, school t-shirt paired with pajama shorts, camera off and the confidence of someone attending a UN summit.

"Annie, are you even awake?"

"Of course, Mom. The teacher marked me present - that's what matters."

The pandemic did more than just cancel school picnics; it reprogrammed our children. They became indoor creatures. Moving from bed to desk (or just staying in bed). School meant logging in, and meals meant yelling "Mom!" from across the room.

It also gave birth to a new superpower – ordering everything online. What started as a safety measure soon turned into a full-blown lifestyle.

Like most families, we too had our lockdown phase of sudden talents.

"We whipped coffee like it owed us money."

"Baked enough cakes to start a home bakery."

"Followed YouTube chefs like they were Nobel laureates."

Annie, who once needed help boiling water, was now plating pasta with basil leaves for "presentation." It was adorable... and mildly terrifying.

But as with all good things, the effort faded - the habit, however, stuck. Only now, instead of cooking, everything started arriving at our doorstep. Annie orders like she's managing a restaurant: "Mom, I've added three things to the cart. Just approve and pay." And if I dare suggest walking to the store next door, she looks at me like I've just asked her to climb Everest... "Why would I walk when Blinkit exists?"

Annie now orders almost everything online. The other day, she was craving avocado toast. I thought I'd be the hero. I stepped out and hunted for the perfect avocado, went to four different places, poked a dozen of them, and came back with something resembling a wrinkled mango.

In the meantime, Annie: "I ordered one online. Arriving in 7 mins. It has 4.8 stars."

It was perfect. She even showed me how to tell if it's ripe via YouTube.

I realized I was not just parenting in the digital age. I was a fossil trying to raise a robot. Post-COVID, there was no comeback. The digital world wasn't a phase; it became their habitat.

That was the moment it hit me - this isn't just about my daughter changing. It's a full-blown generational shift. And suddenly... I felt this wave of empathy for my own parents.

Maybe my parents had the same expression watching me navigate Windows 98 like a tech goddess. Now, it's my turn to blink in confusion while Annie tells Alexa to play "a vibe."

Then came the next revolution - AI. If COVID made them lazy, AI made them unstoppably efficient. Reading books, collecting references, or making notes for any assignment? Gone! Replaced by a few clicks, a Chatbot, and a perfectly formatted answer. No library card required. At least back then, they used to come to us – the wise, wrinkled humans – for help.

"Ma, how do I start an essay?"

Now? They ask ChatGPT – their guru, therapist, life coach, and moral support system. And I just get called in to double-check the printer. I used to be the encyclopedia. Now I'm just tech support, or worse, a delivery agent with emotional damage.

Face-to-face conversations have taken a back seat. Now our home sounds like this: "Check your WhatsApp."

"But you're sitting right here!"

"Yeah, but I sent it. Please reply."

Sometimes, Annie texts me from the same room: "Ma, can we eat now?"

I reply: "Yes, come to the kitchen. Also, bring your own plate."

Everything must be typed, shared, or screenshot, preferably with a timestamp and emoji as evidence.

"Didn't I tell you?"

"Nope. Show me the message."

Apparently, my actual mouth, moving in real-time, is no longer a trusted source of communication. Words spoken aloud vanish into the air, but a text? A text is sacred. Sometimes I wonder if I should start texting Annie from across the table – not to communicate, just to be believed.

Just when I felt I was finally catching up – managing Zoom classes, online homework submissions, and even troubleshooting the Wi-Fi like a pro – I genuinely thought I'd nailed digital code, but language itself evolved.

Annie no longer speaks English. She speaks "Gen Z-ese" – a fast-paced, emoji-rich dialect where every sentence is a puzzle.

I once overheard her say, "This teacher gives such NPC energy, but low-key slays when she's mad."

I blinked like a malfunctioning modem.

NPC? Slay? What happened to "nice" and "strict"?

When I asked Annie what it meant, she patted my head like I was a confused pet. "NPC is like... a background character, Ma. And slay is a compliment."

Oh, wonderful. So the teacher is irrelevant, but killing it. Glad we cleared that up.

One day, she said, "That outfit is a whole vibe."

I said, "No beta, it's just a kurta and jeans."

She looked at me with the kind of pity usually reserved for dial-up internet.

Now everything is a mood, a vibe, or an era.

I can't just be tired – I'm "in my burnt-out era."

I can't enjoy music – I must say, "This song hits different."

Even feelings are expressed in abbreviations: "SMH, IDK, LOL, TBH, ..."

Sometimes I wonder if she's texting me or diagnosing me.

She throws "Slay, Queen!" around so much, I half expect to hear it when I fold laundry.

Bhindi sabzi? Slay.

Watered the plants? Slay.

Didn't burn the toast? Slay.

I smile, nod, and pretend to understand.

Then I secretly Google it all later in private mode, of course.

This is not a complaint – well, maybe a little – it's just my humble attempt to understand the evolving species that once called me "Mumma" and now calls me "bruh."

And don't even get me started on their photography style.

Annie and her friends click pictures with their faces covered by their phones, standing in front of a mirror like they're part of a witness protection program.

Who does that?

During our time, the goal was simple – a clear face, a good angle, and anything to look taller, slimmer, and album-worthy. Now, apparently, the more of your face you hide, the cooler you are.

I once asked Annie why she doesn't smile properly in her photos – she said, "Because it's a vibe, Mom."

A vibe?? I spent 6 weekends doing a photography course - rule of thirds, light angles, the golden hour and now I need lessons from my own child on how to pose like I'm hiding from the paparazzi.

And that's not all. You try standing next to them for a

photo and casually put your hand on their shoulder.

"Ugh, Mom! Don't touch me, it looks weird!"

Weird? I gave birth to you, and now my arm is ruining your aesthetic?

Even clicking pictures now comes with a hidden rulebook.

Smile? Maybe.

Look natural? No.

Don't blink. Don't breathe.

And definitely, don't touch them.

Honestly, it feels like a modelling agency run by moody cats.

No matter how hard we chase their pace, there will always be a moment - that quiet, funny, humbling moment - where we realise: We've become them.

The "you-don't-get-it" generation. And maybe that's the beauty of it. Because the goal isn't to keep up - it's to stay grounded. To keep dancing to our own 90's playlist, ask questions proudly, laugh at ourselves often, and most importantly – not lose our own story while trying to understand theirs.

Let the kids zoom ahead with AI and acronyms. We'll be right here, following with love, a little sass, and very comfortable footwear.

Because isn't that what our parents did for us?

They watched us stumble through floppy disks, boy bands, and mobile phones – staying close, even when they didn't fully understand our world.

Now it's our turn to walk a few steps behind, smiling through the confusion, loving them anyway – just as fiercely. And maybe one day, when our kids become parents, they'll hear their own children say,

"You just don't get it."

And they'll smile too.

After all, every generation gets its turn...

To be slightly outdated – and totally iconic.

~

40

Times Change, Tides Turn

~ Bijal Shah-Chokshi

At 22, Aarin stood outside a fancy glass building in Mumbai, clutching a folder that held his MBA degree. He was wearing his only good suit – borrowed shoes, slightly tight trousers, but a heart full of hope. The degree still smelled like convocation roses.

He had spent years dreaming of handling big portfolios, saying things like "EBITDA" over cappuccinos in boardrooms, and becoming the youngest CFO India had ever seen. Success, for him, had a shape – and it looked like corner offices, business cards, and power suits.

Instead, he found himself selling insurance.

"Financial planning," he would say quickly, correcting anyone who raised an eyebrow.

But deep down, he knew – this wasn't the dream. This wasn't Wall Street. It was staircases in hot buildings, sweaty shirts, and trying to convince skeptical retired uncles to invest in pension plans.

—

Act I: The Detour No One Plans

Jobs were hard to come by that year. A recession had walked in like an unwanted guest at a wedding and decided to stay. Even gold medals and a glowing CV didn't help much.

Aarin tried his best. He smiled at every 'not now' and nodded through every rejection. But the sparkle was fading.

And then came the call that changed everything.

His father, his hero, his guide, the man who once ran a company with calm strength and silly dad jokes, was gone. A heart attack. Sudden. Final.

No warnings. No goodbyes.

Aarin felt like a rocket that had launched, only to lose its base mid-air. The man he wanted to make proud wasn't there anymore. The footsteps he hoped to follow had vanished.

—

Act II: The Drift

That year, something broke inside Aarin. Not all at once. Just slowly. Quietly.

He stopped attending events. Stopped preparing for interviews. The tie he used to wear with hope started to feel like a rope.

Weekends became long, empty stretches. He would sit at home, scrolling meaninglessly, eating instant noodles, watching shows he barely remembered.

One day, on a dull afternoon, he wandered into a bookstore. No real reason – just the comfort of silence and pages.

The self-help section stood out. Big promises in big fonts:

"Awaken the Giant Within."

"The Power of Now."

"Think and Grow Rich."

He read them all. Some made sense. Some didn't. But they gave him something to hold on to.

Then came a different kind of reading. He found the Bhagavad Gita. Listened to podcasts on mindfulness. Signed up for a free course titled "How to Breathe Properly."

At first, he laughed at it. Then he didn't.

He wasn't rebuilding his resume. He was rebuilding himself.

—

Act III: The Climb and the Quiet

By the time he turned 28, things had shifted a little.

He found a new job. Still in finance. Still no corner office. But the numbers made sense again. His team respected him. He got a small raise. Then a bigger role.

The dream wasn't dead – just delayed.

But his personal life was still quiet. Too quiet.

Friends were getting married, moving cities, throwing housewarming parties, and sharing couple selfies with hashtags like #ForeverUs and #LifeGoals.

Aarin, meanwhile, was learning to live alone.

He tried cooking biryani. It became pulao.

He bought a guitar. After six weeks, he could play "Happy Birthday."

He binged shows with Maggi and jokes for company.

He even joked that he was in a relationship with the Amazon delivery guy, who came every other day.

Lonely? Sometimes.

Peaceful? Slowly, yes.

There was no pressure to impress. No constant comparison. Just time – to think, to read, to heal.

He learned to enjoy his own company.

—

Act IV: The Turn of the Tide

At 34, something shifted again.

He met Meera at a friend's get-together. She laughed at his Excel jokes. Hated coriander. Loved long drives. And had a playlist called "Songs for Minor Existential Crises."

They clicked.

They dated.

Then married.

Life stopped being poetic. It became practical and packed.

Mornings began with diaper changes, not alarms. Groceries replaced graphs. Evenings were about doctor visits, not deadlines.

But joy came in new forms – soft lullabies, baby giggles, messy cakes, and bedtime stories that ended with Aarin snoring before his daughter did.

Professionally, he was where he once dreamt of being.

Personally, he was somewhere he never imagined – but now, couldn't imagine living without.

Work-life balance?

Some days, it worked.

Some days, nothing worked.

But he learned: that's life. You juggle. You drop things. You laugh. You try again.

Times Change. Tides Turn.

On his 40th birthday, Aarin stood on a beach near Mumbai.

The breeze was warm. His daughter was holding his hand – her fingers sticky with ice cream. They watched the waves move in and out, slowly, endlessly.

He smiled.

At 22, he believed success meant a glass cabin.

At 30, he thought healing came from books.

At 35, he believed love would arrive like magic.

At 40, he knew the truth: all of it was real. And all of it was just one part of the bigger story.

Life hadn't gone as planned. But that was the plan.

Each twist, each tide, had reshaped him. Like the waves that slowly carve the shore, time had softened him, strengthened him, taught him.

He bent, but didn't break.

He lost, but also found.

He stumbled, but never stopped.

As he watched his daughter chase waves, Aarin whispered a quiet promise to himself:

"Dreams may detour. People may depart. Life may throw its tides. But if you keep walking, the shore never really disappears."

And with that, he turned to follow her, laughing as the sea soaked their feet.

~

41[1]

~

1 Fill these pages with 'Your Time, Your Tide'. Submit your story to us at hello@twagaa.com, Subject: Submission 'Time & Tide'. The best stories will be compiled and published in an anthology.

~

About The Authors

Bhavini Furia, *Family Physician & Cosmetologist*
Bhavini Furia, a family physician and cosmetologist, describes herself as a dreamer sustained by stories. Books have long been her escape, and seeing the enthusiasm of amateur writers around her finally inspired her to pick up the pen and transform private imaginings into written form.
Email: bhavinif77@gmail.com

Arati Raval, *Screenwriter*
Arati Raval is a perpetually overwhelmed Mumbai-based screenwriter, fluent in Bollywood references and 4 other languages. Her deep love for writing and travel fuel each other. Recognised by Filmfare and the Screenwriters Association, she writes for India's leading producers and platforms while raising an energetic son with her actor-husband.
Web: instagram.com/aratiraval
Email: aratiraval@gmail.com

Manisha Divan, *Self Employed*
Manisha Divan, once soaring the skies as cabin crew and now a spirited self-employed professional, lives life in full color. A family anchor, loyal friend, and die-hard coffee lover, she finds joy in non-fiction books, old Hindi tunes, sweat-soaked workouts, and scribbling poems whenever inspiration playfully strikes.
Web: instagram.com/manisha.divan
Email: mdsurti@rediffmail.com

Avani Shah, *Management Consultant*
Avani Shah, a management consultant, has over two decades of experience advising financial services clients in London and India. A mother to two teenage daughters, she treasures moments of connection, finding joy in good books, seaside walks, and preparing meals for loved ones.
Web: instagram.com/avani._shah_
Email: avsash@gmail.com

Manika Tibriwal, *Chef*
Manika Tibriwal, owner of Dips & Co, enjoys transforming what began as a hobby into a successful business venture. A mother to eight-year-old twin boys, she describes herself as a referee, homemaker, chef, and caterer, while drawing inspiration from thriller and comedy films for her creative endeavours.
Web: instagram.com/dipsnco
Email: bmanika23@gmail.com

Yūgen, *Homemaker*
Yūgen invites readers into spaces of calm and reflection where meaning lives beyond words. Drawing from nature's rhythms and intuition's whispers, their writing emerged from a persistent inner calling rather than intention, offering quiet opportunities to breathe, feel, and discover deeper calm.
Email: ankitabansal2020@gmail.com

Madhuja Banerjee, *Senior Vice President, Jiostar*
Madhuja Banerjee, a media professional and creative leader at a leading entertainment channel, considers herself a storyteller at heart. She combines her passion for history, art, travel, and writing to craft engaging content, drawing inspiration from every journey and ancient exploration.
Email: madhujastar@gmail.com

Archana Maru Nanda, *Chartered Accountant, Aditya Birla Group*
Archana Maru Nanda, a Chartered Accountant and Head of Finance at Aditya Birla Group, considers herself a global citizen. Born in India, raised in the UK, and having worked across four continents, her interests range from Kathak dancing to rock climbing and financial literacy advocacy.
Web: linkedin.com/in/archana-maru-nanda-3099a11/
Email: archana.maru@gmail.com

Dr. Vani Parekh, *Ophthalmologist*
Dr. Vani Parekh, an ophthalmologist, was born and raised in Delhi and is now settled in Mumbai. A mother of two, she currently practises at Bharatiya Arogya Nidhi Hospital, combining her medical expertise with dedication to family life in the bustling city.
Email: vaniparekh27@gmail.com

Monaaz Bamji, *Full time mum*
Monaaz Bamji, an ex-auditor and chartered accountant, is now a full-time mother to her seven-year-old. Always inspired by people, places, and cultures, she draws her greatest inspiration from her daughter, who unlocks her imagination as never before, while bringing essence to her creative work.
Email: mnb11@hotmail.com

Nily Mehta, *Freelance Consultant*
Nily Mehta, a freelance consultant with a diverse professional background in Corporate Communication and Branding, has served multinationals and investment banking companies. A Master's degree holder and former postgraduate lecturer, her free-spirited nature fuels passions for singing, travel, and creating relatable, intriguing content.
Web: instagram.com/nilymehta/
Email: nilymehta@gmail.com

Kaushal Patel, *Entrepreneur & Author*
Kaushal Patel, father to two daughters, best friend to his wife, is the co-founder of a fragrance brand. After a 19-year stint as a Corporate Banker, he embarked on fulfilling his dreams of building brands and writing, having published the thriller 'Never Say Never' while living in Mumbai.
Web: instagram.com/kaushalpatel19/
Email: kaushal77patel@gmail.com

Kajal Mehra, *Homemaker*
Kajal Mehra, a professionally qualified chemical engineer, has 14 years' industry experience and is now a dedicated homemaker and full-time mother. She expresses creativity through black and white sketches, watercolours, and writing, while maintaining an avid reading habit and passion for travel.
Web: howgrowingupmatters.com
Email: kajs_m@yahoo.com

Mamta Agarwal, *Homemaker*
Mamta Agarwal, a post-graduate with a diploma in software engineering, has explored diverse career paths – content creation, coding, and talent acquisition – before taking a sabbatical. Now a devoted mother of two, she focuses on her passions while embracing life's opportunities with wonder..
Web: instagram.com/mamta_agarwal09
Email: mamtaagarwal406@gmail.com

Chandni Bhatnagar, *Ex-Indian Coast Guard*
Chandni Bhatnagar, a retired Indian Coast Guard Commandant, is a decorated maritime leader and the first woman to head a Maritime Rescue Coordination Centre. With a record of saving over 1,400 lives at sea, she inspires through her courage, leadership, and storytelling, championing resilience and purpose beyond the uniform.
Web: linkedin.com/in/chandnibhatnagar1/
Email: chandnibhatnagar1@gmail.com

Nirali Hathi, *Homemaker*
Nirali Hathi, a passionate storyteller, believes stories exist everywhere – in city streets, theatre wings, and kitchen tables. A former journalist with The Times of India Group covering art, theatre, and civic affairs, she's a curious traveller and lifelong word-lover who celebrates expression through multiple creative outlets.
Web: linkedin.com/in/nirali-hathi/
Email: hathi.nirali@gmail.com

Krina Gala, *Director, Suditi Industries*
Krina Gala, mother to a spirited 10-year-old chess enthusiast, is a storyteller at heart and a director at Suditi Industries. Rooted in Kutch, she draws inspiration from its heritage and her love for painting, weaving imagination, tradition, and life's quiet lessons into heartfelt narratives and creative expression.
Web: instagram.com/krins85
Email: krins85@gmail.com

Kruti Sharma, *Entrepreneur and Corporate Trainer - POSH / Soft Skills / Compliance*
Kruti Sharma, a dedicated POSH trainer, skilled facilitator, and passionate law student, specialises in soft skills and compliance training. She inspires individuals to stand for justice, using knowledge and courage to shape safer, more inclusive futures through her professional and educational pursuits.
Web: linkedin.com/in/krutisharma
Email: kruti.sharma@gmail.com

Dr. Usha Jayachandran, *Development Economist, Child Rights Consultant*
Dr. Usha Jayachandran, a development economist, has over 30 years' experience in child rights, focusing on child labour and primary education. A trained light-classical singer, lyricist, and artist, she's worked with UNICEF, UNDP, and state governments and has authored the Maharashtra and Uttarakhand State Human Development Reports.
Email: ujchandran@gmail.com

Vandana Narang Lund, *Founding Member & Communications Specialist, Artheart*
Vandana Narang Lund, founder member and Communications Specialist at Artheart, has a creative mindset and passion for life. Her hobbies include reading, writing, journaling, cooking, travelling, and Warli art, combining vast public relations experience with personal growth and creative expression.
Email: vbnarang@yahoo.com

Anjana Chabria, *Psychotherapist/Counsellor*
Anjana Chabria, a psychotherapist and school counsellor, wears many hats at 57 – proud single mother, cancer warrior, and dedicated professional. Life's challenges have deepened her empathy and sharpened her insight, which she pours into helping others with her mantra: one day at a time.
Email: anjanachabria@gmail.com

Parizad Srivastava, *Business Strategy Advisor & Author*
Parizad Srivastava, an accomplished author, certified mindset coach, and nonprofit leader, is passionate about empowering communities and driving social change. She lives in the USA with her family, and combines storytelling with her commitment to making a meaningful difference.
Web: instagram.com/manifestwithparizad/
Email: parizadmylog@gmail.com

Gayatri Hingorani, *Corporate Communications*
Gayatri Hingorani heads Corporate Communications at a leading engineering company, where she drives brand visibility and CSR. Beyond the corporate world, she pursues her passion for creative writing. Her poetry and prose have been featured in multiple publications; most recently, she authored a children's book dedicated to her mother.
Email: gayatrih@gmail.com

Zeyd Ladha, *Businessman & Writer*
Zeyd Ladha, a Mumbai-based engineer-turned-author and businessman, has penned two award-winning books at the Asian Literary Society. With a voice that's optimistic, empathetic, and observant, he believes in literature's power to inspire while weaving themes of positivity and self-love into his work.
Web: facebook.om/zeyd.ladha
Email: zeyd.speed@gmail.com

Amit Suri, *Business - Communication Design & Book Publishing*
Amit Suri, co-founder of a design studio and a publishing house, blends technical expertise, management insight, and creativity with business acumen. With experience in the merchant navy, consulting, and startups, he enjoys meeting like-minded people to collaborate for personal and professional growth.
Web: irustima.com
Email: irustima@gmail.com

Kinjal Mehta, *Master Numerologist & Certified Tarot Reader*
Kinjal Mehta, a Chartered Accountant turned spiritual coach, explores occult science modalities, including tarot, Pythagorean numerology, and crystal healing. An astrophile deeply fascinated by the universe's mysteries, she combines professional expertise with a passion for spirituality and creative expression while working as a real-estate channel partner.
Email: sheth.kinjal@gmail.com

Dr. Ekta Bhatia, *Neuro-Developmental Physical & Behavioural Therapist*
Dr. Ekta Bhatia, a neurodevelopmental physiotherapist and behavioural therapist, has spent 18 years helping babies, children, and families turn small steps into big milestones. Equal parts science and soul, this mother of two spots patterns others miss and gently rewrites them with curiosity and compassion.
Web: ektaruralfoundation.com
Email: ektaruralfoundation@gmail.com

Saloni Chheda, *Creative Director, The Art Maison*
Saloni Chheda, Creative Director of The Art Maison, is born and brought up in Mumbai. After studying Masters in Public Health and working in the field, she started her art and craft business while embracing motherhood, artwork, and discovering new sides of creativity through learning and exploration.
Web: instagram.com/theartmaison
Email: sbsavla12@gmail.com

Manasvi Mehta, *Dentist*
Manasvi Mehta, a dentist and mother, juggles professional responsibilities with family life. Her emotions and expressions flow naturally onto paper, and she's particularly interested in exploring how the digital world affects human connections and family relationships in contemporary society.
Email: manumehta65@gmail.com

Jay Solanki, *Brand Consultant*
Jay Solanki, a brand consultant, calls himself a "brand gynaecologist". He is an engineer by education, a storyteller by passion, and a Gujarati by default. Working with FMCG startups, his participation in product launches has helped birth over 200 new brands across his entrepreneurial journey.
Web: jaysolanki.in
Email: jaysolanki@gmail.com

Payal Shah, *Head of Department, Utpal Shanghvi Global School - Juhu*
Payal Shah, Head of Department at Utpal Shanghvi Global School, holds Master's degrees in Literature, Education, and Commerce and is pursuing a PhD in Education. With over 21 years of experience, she combines academic depth and heartfelt storytelling, finding beauty in life's quiet moments to inspire reflection, connection, and growth.
Web: instagram.com/payal.shah.3912/
Email: payalshahusgs@gmail.com

Vijay Lalla, *Stock Market Trader*
Vijay Lalla, an entrepreneur, stock market trader, and social worker, lives in Mumbai. Father to a teenage daughter learning art and design, he loves helping children with learning while combining his business acumen with community service and creative storytelling pursuits.
Email: vijaylalla777@gmail.com

Ami Dedhia, *Graphic Designer*
Ami Dedhia, a passionate graphic designer and owner of fashion brand Arhaworld, lives with an open heart for life's simple joys. A mother of two energetic boys, she embraces creativity through travel, dance, books, and everyday beauty while balancing work and motherhood with a spirit of positivity.
Web: varadastudio.com
Email: varadastudio@gmail.com

Bijal Pratik Shah, *Chartered Accountant*
Bijal Pratik Shah, a professionally qualified Chartered Accountant, is a full-time, hands-on mother to her spirited seven-year-old. A passionate lover of dance, art, and books, she's a dreamer with vivid imagination who finds joy in life's simple pleasures and treasured moments with family and friends.
Web: instagram.com/bijal_as
Email: bijalpratik@gmail.com

Meghana Chandrachud, *Business, Beauty Products*
Meghana Chandrachud grew up in Mumbai, surrounded by the fragrances of essential oils that sparked a lifelong love for their therapeutic magic. Today, she co-runs à La Naturelle, a natural salon and spa brand, with her husband. A mother of two, she treasures travel, storytelling, and time spent by the sea.
Web: instagram.com/meghanachandrachud
Email: chandrachudmeghana@gmail.com

Anannya Sane, *Student*
Anannya Sane, a finance student, Hindustani classical vocalist, and Kathak dancer, has a flair for storytelling. A Gold recipient of the International Award for Young People, her multidisciplinary passion and artistic sensitivity makes her a vibrant creative voice
Web: linkedin.com/in/anannya-sane-661310283/
Email: anannya.s.sane@gmail.com

Shreya Khosla, *Chartered Accountant*
Shreya Khosla, a chartered accountant, has a passion for writing and sharing experiences. She believes the pen is mightier than the sword and that the right words can create a huge difference in the world through meaningful storytelling and professional expertise.
Email: raizadashreya@gmail.com

Nidhi Shah, *Teacher*
Nidhi Shah, a postgraduate degree in Business Finance and Foreign Trade, is now a proud value education teacher and mother of twins. After a decade in multinational pharmaceuticals and an entrepreneurial journey, she nurtures her passion for reading, writing, and sketching while bringing joy to students.
Web: instagram.com/nidhi1809
Email: nbjshah@gmail.com

Rita Choudhari, *Art Educator*
Rita Choudhari, MBA in Marketing, is an art educator passionate about painting and creativity. Born in Pune, settled in Mumbai, she is a spirited sports enthusiast who loves cricket and throwball. Rooted in Jain values, she enjoys reading, traveling, photography, and discovering new passions that inspire her.
Email: rcartist78@gmail.com

Bijal Shah-Chokshi, *Freelance Content Curator & Academician*
Bijal Shah-Chokshi, an academician, marketing professional, and content curator, works across platforms with a strong belief in content pedagogy. With 15+ years as publisher of 100+ books, she now writes, researches, and edits content rooted in mythology, life skills, and education.
Web: linkedin.com/in/bijals/
Email: s.bijal@gmail.com

Afterword

As this anthology draws to a close, what remains is not just the stories themselves but the spirit in which they were written and shared. Each page carries a fragment of memory, a glimpse of imagination, and a heartbeat of lived experience. Together, they form a chorus of voices that remind us of life's ebb and flow – its joys, its struggles, its silences, and its celebrations.

More than a book, *TIME & TIDE* has been a journey of collaboration. Writers came together as individuals and emerged as a community, discovering that the act of creating side by side forges bonds that endure. The names bound in these pages will remain here for all time, a reminder of what we can achieve when imagination and togetherness meet.

May these stories travel far, spark conversations, and keep inspiring long after the final page is turned.

For time will never stop, and more tides shall return soon.

If you have an interesting story to tell, bring it to us.

We'll help you get published!

~

hello@twagaa.com

TWAGAA

[**T**ogether **W**e **A**re **G**reat, **A**mazing & **A**wesome!]

Acknowledgements

With heartfelt gratitude, we acknowledge Jamnabai Narsee School – not merely as an institution of learning, but as a vibrant platform where its people come together as communities, to collaborate and create.

Our sincere thanks to the school's trustees, Shri Jairaj Thacker and Shri Sujay Thacker, whose vision continues to nurture generations, and to the enterprising principal, Ms. Sonali Gandhi, whose leadership of the school's book club has become the cradle where ideas and imagination bloom.

Most of all, we extend our deepest appreciation to the 40 writers who poured their hearts into these pages. By entrusting TWAGAA with your stories, you have gifted us not just words, but worlds. This anthology is as much yours as it is ours — a timeless keepsake of creativity, courage, and community.

May your tribe thrive!